Cultural China Series

*Hang Jian & Guo Qiuhui*

# Chinese
# Arts & Crafts

## History, Techniques and Forms

*Translated by Zhu Youruo & Song Peiming*

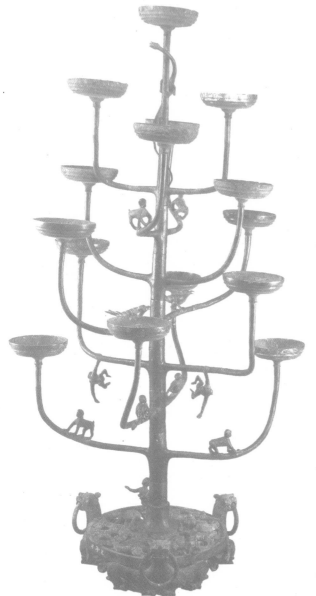

CHINA
INTERCONTINENTAL
PRESS

**图书在版编目（CIP）数据**

中国传统工艺／杭间，郭秋惠著；朱攸若，宋佩铭译.—北京：
五洲传播出版社，2006.10（2008.5重印）
ISBN 978-7-5085-0963-1

I.中... II.①杭... ②郭... ③朱... ④宋... III.工艺美术
史－中国－英文 IV.J509.2

中国版本图书馆CIP数据核字（2006）第093902号

**中国传统工艺**

著　　者　杭　间　郭秋惠
译　　者　朱攸若　宋佩铭
图片提供　杭　间　郭秋惠　盛元富
责任编辑　吴娅民
整体设计　田　林
出版发行　五洲传播出版社（北京海淀区北小马厂6号　邮编：100038）
电　　话　8610-58891281（发行部）
网　　址　www.cicc.org.cn
承 印 者　北京华联印刷有限公司
版　　次　2006年10月第1版
印　　次　2008年5月第3次印刷
开　　本　720×965毫米　1/16
印　　张　10印张
字　　数　62千字
印　　数　5001-9500册
定　　价　90.00元

# Contents

Preface / 1

History and Background of the Traditional Arts and Crafts of China / 9

Arts and Crafts during the Primitive Society / 10

Arts and Crafts during the Xia, Shang and Zhou Dynasties / 12

Arts and Crafts during the Spring and Autumn Period and the Warring States Period / 15

Arts and Crafts during the Qin and Han Dynasties / 18

Arts and Crafts during the Six Dynasties / 21

Arts and Crafts during the Sui, Tang and Five Dynasties / 25

Arts and Crafts during the Song, Liao, Jin and Yuan Dynasties / 29

Arts and Crafts during the Ming and Qing Dynasties / 33

Arts and Crafts in the Field of Utensil / 41

Ceramics / 42

Bronze Ware / 48

Lacquer / 54

Arts and Crafts in the Field of Apparel / 59

Embroidery / 60

Printing and Dyeing / 66

Silk Weaving / 69

Arts and Crafts in the Field of Furnishings / 75

Furniture / 76

Gold and Silver Ware, Glassware, Enamelware / 81

Bamboo Carving, Wood Carving, Ivory Carving / 89

## Arts and Crafts in the Field of Adornment / 97

Jade Artwork / 98

Paper-cut / 103

New Year Picture / 107

## Arts and Crafts in the Field of Entertainment / 111

Toy / 112

Kite / 116

Puppet / 120

Silhouette / 124

## Arts and Crafts in the Field of Commerce / 129

Shop Sign / 130

Packaging / 132

## Legends concerning Traditional Arts and Crafts of China / 137

Yanshi and His Puppets / 140

Lu Ban, a Carpenter Consecrated by Artisans of All Crafts / 140

The Legend of Ganjiang and Moye / 141

The Legend of Brother Kilns / 142

Origin of Kesi Silk / 144

Gourd-shaped Porcelain Canteen and the Yue's Troops / 144

Qiu Changchun, the Forefather of Jade Carving in Beijing / 146

Gong Chun Teapot and Lotus-and-toad Teapot / 147

The Beauty Offered for Sacrifice / 148

Legend about Ceramics with Multicolored Glaze / 148

Origin of Bowl Bottom / 149  Origin of Wax Printing / 150

Bodiless Lacquer Ware Created by Shen Shaoan / 151

## Appendix: A Brief Chronology of China / 153

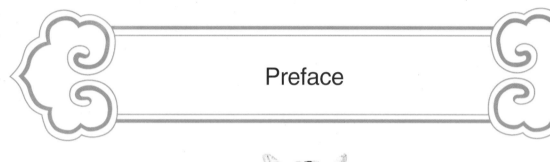

# Preface

The traditional arts and crafts of China have won unique good reputations in the history of the material culture of the various nationalities in the world. Since Zhang Qian (?-c. 114 B.C.) of the Han Dynasty served as an envoy abroad to the Western Regions (a Han Dynasty term for the area west of Yumenguan, including what is now Xinjiang and parts of Central Asia) and the gradual formation of the Silk Road, the traditional arts and crafts of China have been introduced in an unfailing way to the Middle East first via the Central Asia and the Western Asia and then to Europe and the five continents and four oceans. At the time when other nationalities intruded or disorders caused by continuous military operations, Chinese craftsmen in the successive dynasties of past ages could often survive by virtue of one single skill and became emissaries for diffusing the culture of different nationalities. In the traditional Chinese philosophy, Chinese ancient thinkers started, as early as in the first century, to use handicraft skills to compare to and interpret various kinds of considerations in the ways of running a state or looking at life.

All this is related to the unique geographic location of China and its farming culture that was formed continuously for a very long time.

The mainland of China possesses a long coastline but its source of civilization, the Central Plains (comprising the middle and lower reaches of the Yellow River), goes deep into the inland. The three earliest systems of state power in China, the Xia Dynasty, the Shang Dynasty and the Western Zhou Dynasty, all emerged in the inland. For the nationalities that grew up on plains and in mountain areas, cultivation and irrigation of land were the most important ways of existence. As a result, the astronomical calendar, the fabrication of farming tools, and the ethical concept of how to get along well with others all developed on such a premise.

It was this kind of life and the style of art in the agricultural farming society that decided the special features of the traditional arts and crafts of China. Its workmanship surrounded the practice of tilling the farm by men and spinning and weaving by women as well as the way of starting to work at sunrise and to rest at sunset. The initial state of all articles and utensils was closely related to the purpose of different uses. They should be convenient and simple for use, having the wisdom of fitting in with agricultural civilization. Even at its top-level, i.e. the arts and crafts for court use and those for scholars, the vestiges of practical use and tradition of simplicity were still maintained. Its decorative style was natural. Within the vision of natural economy, hills and waters, animals and plants were the main patterns and ornaments. Absurd or ferocious decorations were scarcely seen. Instead they were full of optimistic spirit and progress making.

The Chinese traditional ethics has an argument "Riding a hobby saps one's will to make progress," which was used to oppose "diabolic tricks and wicked craft" so as to hold in check excessive development of skills that had no practical value. The influence of this idea has made the arts and crafts of China develop along the orientation of functionalism for thousands of years without having made waste to the society but having made workmanship develop to the extreme in the farming society instead. Nevertheless, it has also brought about certain conservation as when skills reach certain level, they will cause certain check and hesitation to the advance of social and scientific progress.

On the whole, the tradition of Chinese arts and crafts, however, is worth praising. It has left us abundant cultural heritage, including a lot of man-made articles and wisdom of life.

*Happy Farmers*, a New Year picture of Yangliuqing, depicting the happy rural life in the traditional society of China.

The wisdom implied in the traditional arts and crafts of China can be summed up in the following six aspects:

The first aspect is "to value life and to use objects." It means emphasis should be laid on man's life, all man-made objects should be under control and for all skills the first priority should be given to human beings. This is what we call "people-oriented" today. This aspect is of great importance to the development of the traditional arts and crafts of China. Maybe someone will say that there is nothing strange for this idea as arts and crafts are for people's use and man must be regarded as the main body. Yet such a simple issue like this once had a history with many twists and turns in Europe. After the Industrial Revolution in Britain, as the batch production with machines lowered the production cost and brought about the cheapest products, many people spoke highly of machine production and cheered for the achievements of the Industrial Revolution. However, before long when people found the products turned out by machines were all exactly the same, poorly and hastily manufactured, they began to be discontented with machine-made products, thinking that they denied man's individuality and that it was a compulsory way of life for all people to use the same articles roughly made. On the other hand, to the producers of the batch production in the entire large industrial society, the division of labor along the assembly line was very elaborate and human beings became only a part of the machines. During the whole process of work, there was not any slightest delight worth mentioning. It was not like the traditional manual labor which could give you a feeling of closeness to the natural materials, touching them with your fingers and thinking of them while you were making. When working in the rhythm of agricultural economy, people had a kind of natural delight to work in the country. That was why William Morris (1834-1896), a utopian socialist and idealist in design, appeared in Europe in the 19th century.

At the very beginning, the traditional Chinese arts and crafts gave full considerations to the factor of human beings in making articles for use. Mechanical production in China also already reached a fairly high level in the early stage, particularly at the rudimental stage of capitalism at the end of the Ming Dynasty. At the then Shengze Town of Songjiang (under the jurisdiction of Wujiang of Jiangsu Province today), cotton-weaving industry was already rather developed. Quite a few households had five to ten hand looms and even employed workers to operate them. There was also a clear division of labor between production processes. Nonetheless, this kind of production mode close to capitalist large industry did not develop from quantitative to qualitative change. The seeds of capitalism at the end of the Ming Dynasty, from beginning to end, did not greatly raise the volume of production and make maximum surplus value so that it could be input for extended reproduction and cause revolutionary changes in textile industry just like the Industrial Revolution in Britain through the reform of power in textile industry. Those cotton-weaving proprietors interrelating in innumerable ways with agriculture in the Ming Dynasty input the money they earned from cotton-weaving industry either into agricultural production again or into family construction such as to build houses, to buy land, to take concubine and bear children. Of course, it contains on the one hand the backward side of agricultural economy but on the other hand it also reflects that the feudal society of China laid emphasis on people's life instead of developing mechanical production to extremes. This is closely related to the ancient idea of China to value life, to make man-made things under control, and to give the first importance to human beings in arts and crafts.

Picture of spinning and weaving in *Tiangong Kaiwu* (Exploitation of the Works of Nature).

The second aspect is "to attain practical use and to benefit man." It lays emphasis on utility and people's livelihood. During the Qianlong Reign (1736-1795) of the Qing Dynasty when Western missionaries or diplomatic envoys of various countries came to China, most of the presents they presented to the emperor were playthings, such as chime clocks with robots. It shows that not all the things manufactured in the West at that time were not for practical use or people's livelihood. On the contrary, the objects manufactured in ancient China always laid stress on functional uses. Guan Zhong (725-645 B.C.), a thinker in the Spring and Autumn Period, said something to the effect that wise craftsmen in the ancient time always followed the rule of not wasting their wisdom to make playthings of no use to people. Mo-tzu (c. 468-376 B.C.), a thinker in the Warring States Period, also raised a viewpoint of "doing what is beneficial to people and not doing what is not beneficial to people." Today their views seem very simple but at their time were of great significance. So we can see the Chinese saying of "diabolic tricks and wicked craft" did not become the main trend in the feudal society of China lasting for a few thousand years, from beginning to end. The main trend of the traditional Chinese handicrafts was only the production of those things laying emphasis on practical use, closely related to national economy and people's livelihood, and maintaining humane concerns.

The third aspect is "to give full play to the actual shape of raw materials by careful examination." It stresses the relationship between arts and crafts on the one hand and skills and materials on the other. There were many outstanding examples in this aspect. For instance, when making furniture, skillful carpenters knew how to make use of the characteristics and grain direction of timber to deal with different structures; when making ink stones, good artisans knew how to make use of the natural material quality of a particular piece of stone to shape beautifully into an ink stone; and when carving jade articles, excellent jade artisans knew how to give full play to the "coincidental natural colors" on a piece of jade and carved something with practical purpose according to its special features. These are only small examples of how handicraft articles were made in accordance with their respective uniqueness. From the macroscopic viewpoint, traditional arts and crafts of China paid great attention to materials and technical conditions and designed articles in line with functional requirements.

A simple and unsophisticated garden in the south of the Yangtze River.

When talking about how to design a landscape in his *Xian Qing Ou Ji* (Occasional Verbal Messages to Repose My Digressive Feelings), Li Yu (1610-1680, a famous man of letters at the turn of the Ming Dynasty and the Qing Dynasty) said the essential thing of landscaping was its appropriate entirety. This is a point of great importance. Under the major background of farming society, the Chinese never made any object deviating from the life of farming society and the handicraft articles made at different period of time were basically all harmonious with the way of life. The gilded bronze lamp of Changxin Palace of the Western Han Dynasty is one of the outstanding examples of Chinese traditional handicrafts. It is really an ingenious design to filter the smoke dust by making use of sealed water, to discharge the smoke with flue and to adjust the light by a rotating structure.

The fourth aspect is "to follow nature in an ingenious way." It emphasizes that inspiration should be drawn from nature so as to maintain the harmony between man and nature. In the past people always thought the term "to follow nature" was only an expression commonly used in painting. Actually, it has also run through the traditional arts and crafts of China, following nature and drawing inspiration from nature so that harmony between man-made articles and nature could be maintained. In ancient China, its expression was particularly obvious such as the various bionic lamps and lanterns in the Han Dynasty, the saw invented by master artisan Lu Ban (c. 507-c. 444 B.C.) and the competition of air vehicles (flying kites) between Lu Ban and Mo-tzu. The inspiration of all this was drawn from nature. In addition, the wooden ox and gliding horse

*Changxin Palace Lamp* of Western Han Dynasty, 48 cm high, stored in Cultural Relics Research Institute of Hebei Province.

invented by Zhuge Liang (181-234) mentioned in the *Romance of the Three Kingdoms* for transporting army provisions along the narrow passages in Sichuan Province were also designed with the combination of machinery and bionic shapes. There were many such similar examples in ancient times. Even some instruments for astronomical observation, such as the seismograph invented by Zhang Heng (78-139), a Chinese scientist in the Eastern Han Dynasty, were also made in accordance with some shapes related to nature. *Xiu Shi Lu* (Lacquer in Ancient China), a monograph about lacquer handicraft written in the Ming Dynasty, put forward explicitly the idea of "following nature in an ingenious way." During the Qianlong Reign many luxury goods were made of porcelain in animal shapes. There were even more examples in folklore utensils such as fish-shaped plates, incense bags, cake molds, gate locks, etc. The shapes of animals not only have functional significance but also contain the unique symbols of Chinese folk culture.

The fifth aspect is "to convey truth with skills." It implies that skills also contain ideological factors and attention should be paid to both ideas and articles so that the functional operation and technical labor that seem inferior can be combined with doctrines and theories that seem superior. As early as in the pre-Qin Dynasty, this concept was formed, of which the influence of the Taoist School thought was the greatest. The Confucian School had similar ideas, such as "to

Folk pillow showing a fish with tiger head.

convey truth with writings." Though the relationship between theory and practice was often not properly dealt with in the Chinese history and the trend of looking down upon practice and stressing on theory was widely spread, theory has never been more important than practice in the daily life of ordinary people.

The sixth aspect is "to balance outward grace and solid worth," which means the unification of content and form in nature as well as the unification of function and decoration in handicraft articles. Many examples can be found in the traditional arts and crafts of China. Viewed from the general development of man's culture, decorative art is an aspect of great importance. However, the emphasis of the unification of content and form on the one hand and the unification of function and decoration on the other can avoid the trend of dropping into formalism or paying attention to function exclusively. This is the outcome of the Confucian influence of "balancing outward grace and solid worth." It requests people to maintain forever the orientation of balancing outward grace and solid worth in the respects of way of life, code of conducts and the relationship between man-made articles and man.

What is mentioned above is the wisdom of the traditional arts and crafts basically summed up from the mainstream thoughts of imperial nobles or scholars. However, the wisdom of the handicrafts of ordinary people is more excellent and richer. It has its own independent system often contained in man-made articles, pithy formulas (often in rhyme), legends and stories. Viewed from the process of the ancient history of China, the development of traditional arts and crafts is basically normal and healthy. Though some over-elaborated tastes and likings did occur during some periods in the history, the traditional arts and crafts of China, from the viewpoint of the whole history, were all in conformity with the development of the productivity at that time and expressed temperance and real aesthetic quality and style.

# History and Background of the Traditional Arts and Crafts of China

# Arts and Crafts during the Primitive Society

In the early stage of human society, stone artifacts were the main implements of production. Through the fabrication of stone artifacts man had a better understanding of the effect and significance of hands and thus handicrafts gradually developed. As early as 1,700,000 years ago, at the age of the Yuanmou Man in Yunnan Province, China, the ancients of China began to make rough stone artifacts as implements or weapons for existence. At the time of the Upper Cave Man, that was 17,000 years ago, there were plentiful kinds of stone artifacts and in the respect of technological processing, the technology of drilling, scraping, polishing, and line engraving were already used. The technological fabrication could preliminarily meet the demand of man's material life and the rudiment of decoration also appeared to reflect their aesthetic consciousness. The Upper Cave Man also learned how to drill wood to make fire. The development from preserving kindling material to bore wood to get fire showed

Jade dragon of the Hongshan Culture, collected in Wengniute Prefecture Museum of Inner Mongolian Autonomous Region.

Stone club and millstone in the Neolithic Age.

the great improvement of man's ability for existence. The use of fire made possible all the later crafts, like the invention of pottery and metallurgy, which was of extraordinary significance in the history of development of human culture.

In the process of material selection for stoneware, people found some "beautiful stones" with close grains and sparkling colors. With meticulous processing, they made the stones into ornaments either for carrying with them or being buried with them after death. Thus jade ware craft was developed and gradually became an independent variety of workmanship.

Buildings reflect man's consciousness for settlement. In line with their respective geographic conditions, people of the clan society in ancient China built dwelling places in different styles, semi-underground basement in the northern Yellow River valley and nests on trees in the southern Yangtze River valley. For meeting the demand of dwelling, people also developed carpentry. From the dwellings ruins in Yuyao, Zhejiang, we can see the people there already lived a kind of settled life in houses built with earth and wood seven thousand years ago.

In early days, when processing natural materials, people only changed their appearance but pottery-making changed the nature of clay with fire, which was a development by leaps and bounds. Earthenware not only enriched utensils for daily life but also increased the stability of the settled farming life. After entering patriarchal society, pottery-making was changed from a community undertaking of a clan to a special

Face profile painted pottery pot of the Yangshao Culture in the Neolithic Age, collected in the National Museum of China.

production department controlled by a family. Technology was improved and pottery varieties were increased. Grey pottery, black pottery and white pottery made with china clay all came into being.

The handicraft culture of the ancient times in China formed different regional features with their respective advantages. For instance, the painted pottery of the Yangshao Culture in the north (7,000-5,000 years ago) was well developed, the sculptures of the Hemudu Culture in the south (c. 7,000 years ago) were remarkable, and the Longshan Culture in the eastern region (5,000-4,000 years ago) scored a success in modeling. The handicrafts of the primitive society already had the distinctive feature of making full use of various kinds of skills and attained the unity of practical use and decoration.

## Arts and Crafts during the Xia, Shang and Zhou Dynasties

Starting from the Xia, the Shang and the Western Zhou, China began the replacement of dynasties one after another. Both the Xia and the Shang had official post specially set up to manage handicrafts under the direct control of royal families and nobles. The sacrificial vessels, sacrificial utensils, weapons and valuable articles for daily use needed by the rulers were all fabricated by the handicrafts under the control of officials. Most of the craftsmen in the Shang Dynasty belonged to the respective clan engaged in a special kind of handicraft from generation to generation but a small part of them were slaves transformed from prisoners of war.

Bronze ware was an important handicraft variety in the Shang Dynasty. The bronze ware of the Shang Dynasty had almost all categories with various shapes. For decorative designs, they were of central symmetry or single line patterns, mysterious and solemn. Due to the tendency of drinking prevailing among the ruling class of the Shang Dynasty, the making of drinking vessels was highly developed. As the cost was very high, the bronze ware could only be used by rulers. For the broad masses of slaves, earthenware was still taken as principal articles for their daily necessities. As a result, the pottery-making technique of the Shang Dynasty was also universally developed. There were three kinds of technique to make pottery: wheel, mold and their combination. There was also an internal division of labor for the pottery-making technique and different kilns fired different potteries. China is the first nation in the world to breed silkworms, weave silk fabrics and use lacquer. In the Shang Dynasty, wild silkworms had already been domesticated. The coating of lacquer can prevent wooden articles from rotting and be used for decoration as well. So far as decoration was concerned, the handicraft in the Shang Dynasty was full of strong religious color and its religious significance was more important than aesthetic consciousness.

In politics, the Western Zhou Dynasty practiced three different systems: the system of granting titles and territories to the nobles; the hereditary system; and the hierarchy system of power. The system of rites was greatly stressed, which affected the formation and development of the technology in dress and personal adornment, utensils, palace chambers and horse-drawn carriages of the Zhou Dynasty. In economy, the "nine squares" system of land ownership (one large square divided into nine small ones, the eight outer ones being allocated to slaves who had to cultivate the central one for the owner) was adopted, which expanded the scale of

White pottery *dou* (hollow container) from the Shang Dynasty, a treasure with exquisite patterns of thunder clouds, elegant in style and dignified in shape.

Bronze mask from the Shang Dynasty, unearthed from Sanxingdui in Guanghan City of Sichuan Province in 1986.

Three-in-one *yan* from the Shang Dynasty, a cooking utensil something like a steaming pot.

agricultural production and the collective labor became a scene of showing farming technique. The large number of handicraft slaves captured by the Zhou Dynasty in the process of conquering the Shang Dynasty also provided favorable factors for the development of handicrafts.

According to the *Kao Gong Ji* (The Records of Examination of Craftsmen), the earliest monograph on handicrafts in China, the Western Zhou Dynasty divided social labor into six categories: the nobility, literati and officialdom, craftsmen, traveling merchant, farmer, and needle worker. At that time the division of labor for the handicraft was very elaborate. There were thirty kinds of work in six handicrafts, namely, carpenter, bronzer, tanner, painter, carver, and pottery maker. Division of labor on the basis of specialization had already formed but production was under the unified operation and management of local authorities with raw materials and workshop provided. Coordination of several different professions was needed for manufacturing many objects. For instance, it needed the cooperation of carpenters, bronzers, lacquerers and tanners to manufacture a chariot. So the handicraft was broad in scale and strict in organization.

For meeting the demand of administration with rites, the handicrafts of the Western Zhou Dynasty, such as bronze ware, dyeing and weaving, lacquer ware and jade ware, reflected rigid difference of social strata in quantity, shape, color, lines and grain as well as in their use, showing a feeling of perfect order. For utensils of livelihood, farms tools and weapons, bronze craft was still an important variety at that stage. Many bronze wares had long inscriptions engraved to give an account of the content of offering sacrifices to gods or ancestors, eulogizing somebody's virtues, granting a reward, doing exchanges, getting married, or taking litigation. In decoration, there was a trend of simplicity and plainness rich in a feeling of rhythm. The fabrication and use of primitive porcelain were also rather popular, the technique of applying glaze was obviously improved, and the hardness, moisture absorption and mineral composition were close to later porcelain.

# Arts and Crafts during the Spring and Autumn Period and the Warring States Period

During the Spring and Autumn Period and the Warring States Period, with the integration of the slave system and the gradual establishment and development of the feudal system, handicraftsmen got rid of the slavery of the slave system, their enthusiasm for production was greatly heightened, and the social production obtained greater development. At this period many handicraft articles with exquisite workmanship, beautiful shape and unique creativeness appeared in the field of arts and crafts, such as metallurgy, ceramics, dyeing and weaving and lacquer ware.

During the Warring States Period, iron-smelting industry came into being on the basis of copper metallurgy and China took the lead in the world to enter upon the Iron Age in an

Mirror with the patterns of hunting inlaid with gold and silver from the Warring States Period.

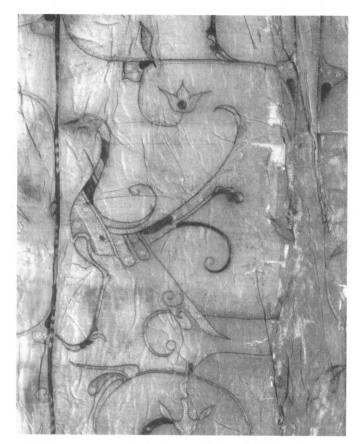

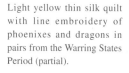

Light yellow thin silk quilt with line embroidery of phoenixes and dragons in pairs from the Warring States Period (partial).

all-around way. There were a great many pottery-making workshops run by the government or by self-employed artisans, all giving first place to gray pottery. Due to the prevalence of elaborate funeral, painted pottery was rapidly developed. As lacquer ware was anticorrosive, moisture-proof, light in weight and good-looking in appearance, its technology also began to develop. The lacquer ware produced in the Kingdom of Chu was the most developed. Due to the development of iron smelting, the improvement of pottery-making and the appearance of lacquer ware, bronze ware stepped into a later stage and was gradually replaced by lacquer ware. The dyeing and weaving technology and production were widely distributed and the most developed areas were in Qi (the present northern Shangdong) and Lu (the present southern Shangdong). Knee-deep clothes and *hufu* (short clothes worn by non-Han nationalities living in the north and west in ancient times) were not mutually exclusive. Knee-deep clothing was a kind of garment with the upper part linked up with the lower part and the lower hem was edged but not slit in the sides. It was the main fashion of that time, continuing up to the Han Dynasty. The *hufu* was originally worn by the nomadic people on the grasslands in the north, having the characteristics of jacket, trousers and boots. Later it was introduced into the Central Plains, improving combat effectiveness and bringing about convenience to life.

With the development of social production, a situation of contention of a hundred schools of thought also emerged in the academic field during the Spring and Autumn Period and Warring States Period. Trends of social thought, art and culture were unprecedentedly prosperous. Various schools of thought, such as Confucianist, Taoist, Mohist and Legalist, had a deep impact on the development of arts and crafts of that time and the later ages as well. For instance, the Confucian School laid emphasis on the unity of content and form; the Taoist School advocated the ethical thought "Great art conceals itself" (that is, a capable man pretends to be stupid in order to avoid jealousy); the Mohist School laid stress on the ideas of "economization" and "Content first, form second;" and the Legalists were against forms but for functions. The hundred schools of thought and their exponents all regarded the handicraft technology as an advanced productivity. They often took skills as examples to expound their respective thought, to make use of objects for giving explicit instructions and to reason things out with implements. It is indeed something rare and deserving praise for the *Kao Gong Ji* , the earliest monograph on handicrafts at that time, to sum up the scientific experiences of various kinds of workmanship and put forward the simple and straightforward handicraft viewpoint. Under the influence of contention of a hundred schools of thought, the workmanship of the arts and crafts during the Spring and Autumn Period and Warring States Period formed the characteristics of clever ideas, new looks and vivacious styles.

At that time, the handicraft industry run by dukes and princes or by self-employed artisans could be found in many

*Kao Gong Ji* (The Records of Examination of Craftsmen).

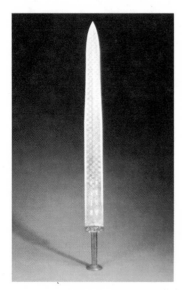

Goujian's bronze sword from the late Spring and Autumn Period, still very sharp today, a masterpiece of the Wu and Yue states.

states. The independent production and development of the various states formed their regional and diversified workmanship. Various states had their respective regional famous products, such as the lacquer ware and leather-making of the Chu State, the swords of the Wu and Yue States, the bows and cross bows of the Han State, the iron-smelting of the Zhao State, the bamboo ware and woodenware of Ba and Shu States, the pottery-making of the Qi State and the jewelry in the southern coastal area. The shape of utensils made in the Chu State was tall and straight and the subject for decoration was of romantic style, full of fantasy; the articles made in the Qin State were of realistic style, simple and unsophisticated; the Zhao State was known for its simplicity and vigorousness; the Zheng State, for its exquisiteness and ingeniousness; the Yan State, for its primitiveness and simplicity; and the Han State, for its refinement and elegance. The handicraft articles made in various states all reflected the strong flavor of their respective style.

# Arts and Crafts during the Qin and Han Dynasties

The period of the Qin Dynasty and the Han Dynasty was a period to establish and consolidate a centralized feudal monarch with multi nationalities united in China. The political system of centralization of the state power required the technologic production under a single command and a grand scale. A segment of a whole can be seen from the world-famous architectures and statues of the Qin Dynasty such as the Great Wall, the tomb of the First Emperor of the Qin Dynasty and his terracotta warriors and horses.

There were two kinds of operation for the arts and crafts in the period of the Qin Dynasty and the Han Dynasty: run by the government and by self-employed artisans. The former was mainly to meet the demands of imperial household and the nobility, the *yamen* (government office in feudal China) at all levels and the army. So the scale was grand, the trades

were numerous, the division of labor was elaborate, the management was perfect, and the funds were abundant. As for the latter, the natural economy of the self-supporting and self-sufficient agricultural society was its important content, i.e. men tilling the farm and women weaving.

Terracotta warriors of Qin Dynasty, unearthed from the tomb of the First Emperor of the Qin Dynasty in Lintong, Shaanxi.

The government-run handicrafts of the Qin Dynasty included mining, smelting and casting, arms and weapons, carriages and chariots, tools and implements, lacquer ware and earthenware. The government, from the central to the local, set up large-scale handicraft administrations. During the Qin and Han period, iron-smelting industry had a great development. With the emergence of the technology of

Eaves tiles of gray pottery gods from the Han Dynasty, the four gods and the central point protruding from the surface, lively and imposing.

well-tempered steel forged for several times, the quality of ironware like weapons and farm tools was improved and social production promoted. In the early stage of the Qin Dynasty, ministerial government was honest and upright, the people were simple and honest, and arts and crafts laid stress on practical use with simple and unadorned shapes. As the rule of the Qin Dynasty lasted for only fifteen years, not too many handicraft articles have been handed down and what was left is mainly bronze ware, lacquer work and earthenware.

In the Han Dynasty, the varieties of handicraft articles grew in number and new creations were made in the aspects of art, technology and materials, so that the unity of practical purpose and aesthetic consciousness was achieved, and one object for multiple uses was invented. For instance, copper lamp is not only convenient for use but can also be used for adornment; and the lacquer case is so cleverly designed that its space can be made full use of. Spinning and weaving was an important handicraft department at this time and thousands of people worked in the government-run workshop. The textiles of the Western Han unearthed at Mawangdui in Changsha, Hu'nan, have many different varieties and the workmanship is of great exquisiteness, representing the high standard of the textile technology of that time. Linzi of Shandong, Chenliu of He'nan and Xiangyi of Hubei were all the famous places of textile production at that time.

The arts and crafts of the Han Dynasty often took the real life and production for themes of decoration, such as feasting, dancing, hunting, assaulting, ploughing and sowing, harvesting, smelting, etc. Due to the trend of turning

*Bi Xie* (a holy beast believed to get rid of evil spirits), carved from bluish white jade from the Western Han collected in Xianyang Municipal Museum, Shaanxi.

Confucianism into a religion in the Han Dynasty, the rise of divination combined with mystical Confucianist belief as well as the prevalence of elaborate funeral, the content of ascending to heaven and becoming immortals, auspicious sign and superstition, and the gods in the four directions prevailed in the ornamental themes. The technique of expression adopted for the ornament was plane silhouette, which was skillful in grasping dynamic and typical characteristics and had the features of simplicity and flexibility as well as vivaciousness and variousness. The composition was full but not in a mess and large in number but not scattered in layout.

During this period, the exchanges and integration between various parts of the country and various nationalities were very lively, forming a unified commercial market at home. As a result, the characteristics of combining craftsmen and merchants and the operation of producing and marketing one's own products all by oneself were formed.

Zhang Qian of the Han Dynasty, an envoy abroad to the Western Regions for two times, opened the Silk Road on the land from Chang'an directly to the Central Asia, the Western Asia and the east coast of the Mediterranean Sea. In addition, the Han Dynasty also opened a land-borne pass to India and the water route on the sea along the coast of China to Japan via Korea. The economic and cultural exchanges between China and other countries were very frequent. China began to export silk fabrics, lacquer ware, ironware and handicraft articles throughout the world.

Black lacquer plate from Western Han, decorated with cloud patterns in scarlet and grayish green lacquer. The three auspicious Chinese characters in the middle written with scarlet lacquer are combined with the patterns, which was very popular in the Western Han and has become the unique form of the decorative patterns of Chinese handicraft.

# Arts and Crafts during the Six Dynasties

During the period of the Six Dynasties, wars occurred frequently in the north but the south was comparatively stable. The shifting of a large number of population and technical strength to the south promoted the exploitation and development of the south. The situation of taking the north as the center of economy and handicraft production for a long time began to change and a new situation was formed for the whole nation to develop in a balanced way.

The Six Dynasties, inheriting upward from the Western Han Dynasty and the Eastern Han Dynasty and handing down to the Sui Dynasty and the Tang Dynasty, was an important transitional period in the handicraft history of China. The turbulence of the society, the sufferings brought about by the war, and the mental agony gave an opportunity to the rise and dissemination of Buddhism to publicize karma and samsara and the rulers also made use of Buddhism to consolidate their rule. As a result, Buddhism was energetically encouraged. In the north, grottos were profusely dug. The well-known Mogao Grottoes in Dunhuang, the Datong Grottoes, and the Luoyang Grottoes are all the pioneering works left from that time. In the south, Buddhist temples were widely built. The various kinds of arts and crafts during that period all had a strong color of Buddhism. Many a brass or copper ware, gold vessel, silverware, carved stone, textile, embroidery and lacquer ware all contained the subject of Buddhism. Lotus and honeysuckle, the main ornament at that time, became the symbols of Buddhism. The prevalence of Buddhism also contributed to and expanded international exchanges. The visit of monks from India and craftsmen from the Western Regions introduced the Indian art compromising the Greek and Persian styles to China and impelled the handicraft culture of China to carry out a new synthesis. Therefore, the religious trend and foreign style of the industrial art are the important handicraft features of the Six Dynasties.

In the ideological sphere, metaphysics prevailed. Supported by the ideology of Lao-tzu (Li Er), Chuang-tzu (Zhuang Zhou) and *The Book of Changes*, metaphysics paid close attention to the reality of personal existence, expounded the special relationship between man and society and between man and nature, and advocated idle talk, mysteries, tranquility and detachment from reality. The "nil" of the metaphysics happens to be coincidental to the "emptiness" of Buddhism. What was reflected in the industrial art was the ornamental subjects of uninhibitedness and noninterference, keeping aloof from worldly things. They

Celadon *zun* (a kind of wine vessel) in lotus shape from the Northern Dynasty with gorgeous pattern and well-rounded shape, a representative work of northern celadon.

were represented by the picture of "Seven Virtuous Persons in Bamboo Grove" joined with bricks and formed an industrial style of delicacy and prettiness as well as sparseness and spaciousness. Brick pictures were particularly used to express sages and men of virtue. Compared with the Han Dynasty, the industrial art of the Six Dynasties was richer in the delight of life and was also penetrated with the color of Buddhism such as lotus, curly grass, rocks and trees. Benefited from the improvement of technological level, the Six Dynasties often made large-scale theme mural integrated with a number of pictures joined with bricks.

By the Six Dynasties, China had entered the porcelain age. Though primitive porcelain came into being as early as in the

*Seven Virtuous Persons in Bamboo Grove*, a mosaic expresses the scene of scholars pursuing personal freedom gathered in a bamboo grove drinking and composing poems in the period of Wei and Jin.

Glass bowl from the Northern Wei.

Shang Dynasty, it was not until the later period of the Han Dynasty that the fabrication technology became basically perfect. Not only is porcelain solid, easy to wash, heat-resisting, and acid- and alkali-resisting but also fine, smooth, warm and moist to the touch, and translucent. All this is in conformity with people's aesthetic requirements. Since then, ceramic has become a main variety in people's household necessities that even can not be completely replaced by the modern products made of glass, plastics, aluminum, etc.

In the respect of dyeing and weaving technology, the figured satin woven in Sichuan was the most famous during the period of Three Kingdoms and the Western Jin Dynasty and the Eastern Jin Dynasty. However, in the Southern Dynasty, the dyeing and weaving technology was also universally developed in the regions south of the Yangtze River and the output of silk weaving products was enormous in Jingzhou and Yangzhou. The veins and grain of silk weaving during the period of the Six Dynasties were no longer irregular and uneven like those made in the Han Dynasty but instead regular waves in geometric pattern were woven.

By this time, handicraftsmen had already obtained independence and freedom to a certain extent. They were allowed to be engaged freely in production and update the technology. In a certain sphere they could also carry out their own handicraft operation so as to promote the development of the varieties of handicraft articles. The invention and improvement of various kinds of implements impelled the

development of social production and life. For instance, during the period of Three Kingdoms, the politician and strategist Zhuge Liang invented the wooden ox and gliding horse, a means of transport in mountainous regions and Ma Jun, a master artisan, invented a farm tool for water conservancy, i.e. the later keel-plate waterwheel, and productivity was greatly improved.

Shoes from the Eastern Jin: the sole woven with flaxen thread and the other parts with silk thread of brown, red, white, black, blue, yellow and green. It is collected in Xinjiang Uygur Autonomous Region Museum.

# Arts and Crafts during the Sui, Tang and Five Dynasties

The period of the Sui Dynasty and the Tang Dynasty was a stage of great prosperity in the ancient society of China. As the reunified multi-national country was further developed and consolidated, the social economy and culture became unprecedentedly prosperous.

During the period of the Sui Dynasty and the Tang Dynasty, the government still controlled the main handicraft departments and the administrative setups were more perfect. The government-run handicraft played a leading role in the respects of scale, organization, division of labor and technology. Many products were sold abroad through tributes, grants and trading and they were also sold at home through the form of monopolized sale. The division of labor

*Musicians on camelback*: Tang-dynasty tri-color figurines.

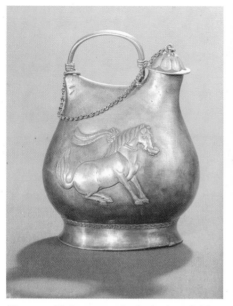

Silver pot with the patterns of a dancing horse holding a cup in its mouth from the Tang Dynasty, collected in Shaanxi Museum.

Bronze mirror from the Tang Dynasty with brown lacquer coated on the back inlaid with a mother-of-pearl dragon coiling in clouds.

was even more elaborate. Artisans of different profession had to receive technical training and study from nine months to four years, for instance, metalsmith for four years; artisan to make musical instrument and chariot, three years; and bamboo artisan, carpenter and lacquerer, one year.

In the Sui and the Tang period, the development of folk handicrafts and the emergency of guild organization further advanced the folk handicrafts with commodity production as their purpose. In addition to farmers' household handicrafts and the handicrafts run by bureaucratic landlord manor, folk handicrafts concentrated gradually towards the city. Handicraft workshops developed rapidly and the types of work in production involved dyeing and weaving, porcelain, lacquer ware and woodenware, gold vessel and silverware, jade ware, smelting and casting, vehicles and boats, papermaking and printing, and grain processing. In the Tang Dynasty, commercial firm organizations something like guilds also emerged to coordinate the internal relations and stipulate the regulations for production and sale, which were recognized and protected by the government. The guild organization greatly affected the social economy, improved universally the social status of the handicraftsmen and marked a new stage of development for the handicraft of China.

Jade cup in the shape of cloud from the Tang Dynasty.

In the Sui Dynasty, the handicrafts of ceramics, dyeing and weaving, and ship-building were comparatively prominent. In the Tang Dynasty, due to the highly developed economy, the liberal state policies, and the frequent exchanges between China and foreign countries, handicraft technology was further developed. Brocade, textile printing and dyeing, ceramics, gold vessel and silverware, lacquer ware and woodenware developed in an all-around way. The ornamental style of this period was different from the simple and unsophisticated characteristics of the Shang, the Zhou, the Han, and the Six Dynasties and began to have the style and features of modern ornament. The ornamental subjects differed from the geometrical style of the primitive society and the realistic or imaginative animal-pattern lines of the Shang Dynasty, the Zhou Dynasty and the Six Dynasties and large numbers of plant lines were adopted instead. They were oriented to the nature and life, rich in strong delight of life, and the general style of the ornamental subjects tended to be pure and fresh, splendid and well-shaped. The technique of ornament and the means of technology were rich and colorful. The ceramic craft used various glaze colors and for glaze application there were many methods, such as glaze splashing, glaze flowing, base winding and glaze winding; the dyeing and weaving handicraft also used several techniques, such as wax printing of figured silk fabrics, twist printing of figured silk fabrics, clip printing of figured silk fabrics, soda printing and rubbing printing; and the lacquer ware used the technique of lacquer inlaid with mother-of-pearl, tracing a design in gold, putting ramie fabrics in between two layers of lacquer, and lacquer carving.

# Arts and Crafts during the Song, Liao, Jin and Yuan Dynasties

As the handicraft level of the Song Dynasty was rather high, obvious development was made in various aspects, such as the development of varieties, the scale of production, the technology of handicrafts, the management and trading. The administrative setups of government-run handicrafts were more unwieldy and the division of labor was more elaborate than the Tang Dynasty. Most of the artisans of the government-run handicrafts were recruited and had personal freedom to a certain extent while the management of the folk handicraft workshop was even more flexible and open. The commerce of the Song Dynasty was well developed, the urban economy became brisk day by day and handicrafts became commodity production universally. In Bianliang (the capital of the Northern Song Dynasty in the present Kaifeng, Henan) and Lin'an (the capital of the Southern Song Dynasty in the present Hangzhou, Zhejiang) shops and stores stood in great numbers, gathering together almost all articles of daily use, and urban handicrafts were very flourishing. The scroll of the *Qingming Shanghe Tu* (Pure Brightness Day on the River) drawn by Zhang Zeduan (1085-1145) of the Northern Song Dynasty showed the busy commercial activities in Bianliang city in a lively and visual representation. There was regular country fair on the outskirts of big cities like Chang'an, Luoyang, Fuzhou, Quanzhou, Yangzhou and Chengdu. Gradually the rural fairs developed into market towns.

The Song Dynasty deserved the title of the "Porcelain Age" as porcelain was the most outstanding of all its handicrafts. Famous kilns were scattered from north to south. The Dingyao Kiln, Ruyao Kiln, Guanyao Kiln, Geyao Kiln

A porcelain pillow from the Dingyao Kiln of the Song Dynasty, a piece of rare ancient porcelain exquisitely made in the shape of a vivacious kid.

Left: Three-foot *xi* (small vessel containing water for washing writing brushes) from the Ruyao Kiln in the Northern Song Dynasty, coated with smooth and lustrous cyan glaze both inside and outside. Right: Inscriptions on the bottom.

and Junyao Kiln were known as the five famous kilns of the Song Dynasty. They created ceramic varieties with their respective characteristics, such as the white porcelain of the Dingyao Kiln, the celadon of the Ruyao Kiln, the light greenish blue porcelain of the Guanyao Kiln, the crackle porcelain of the Geyao Kiln, the transmutation porcelain of the Junyao Kiln and the shadowy blue porcelain of the Jingdezhenyao Kiln. In addition, the simple and straightforward porcelain fired by folk kilns like the Cizhouyao Kiln in the north and the Jizhouyao Kiln in the south was very popular among the people. The ceramic technology of the Song Dynasty achieved unprecedented prosperity by incorporating the great achievements of the successive dynasties. The dyeing and weaving technology of the Song Dynasty was also greatly developed. The varieties of silk weaving were plentiful and the center of silk weaving was in the regions south of the Yangtze River. For the production of lacquer ware, not only did the government have special administrative setups, the fabrication among folk people was also so common that local centers were formed. For the jade carving technique, as the "qiao se" (coincidental natural colors) on the jade was given full play to, gigantic achievements were obtained.

Due to the popularity of the idealist philosophy in the Song Dynasty, the doctrine of "maintaining heavenly principles and restraining people's desires" was greatly

Jade ornament from the Jin Dynasty: flat in shape and partially purplish red.

Carved blue-and-white underglaze red jar with lid from the Yuan Dynasty: simple and vigorous in shape and bright in gradation of decorative patterns.

emphasized. The technology of ceramics, lacquer ware, metalworking and furniture of the Song Dynasty all scored success with simple and unadorned shapes, having the style of refinement and amiableness with little overelaborate adornment. In the Song Dynasty, the establishment of imperial art academy system made drawing emphasized and intervened directed into the fabrication of industrial art. For instance, the handicrafts of embroidery and *kesi* silk were used to express drawing. They became handicraft articles mainly for enjoyment and affected greatly the later industrial art of the Ming Dynasty and the Qing Dynasty.

In 1127, the troops of the Jin Dynasty went southward and conquered Kaifeng. The royal family of the Song Dynasty moved southward and made Hangzhou the capital, which was called the Southern Song Dynasty in the history. At the time of moving southward, the imperial court of the Song Dynasty also brought with it the production technologies and

A gilded silver cockscomb pot from the Liao Dynasty, typically shaped like Khitan nationality's leather bag, its adornment skill and line patterns obviously affected by the inland traditional handicraft.

skilled craftsmen of the north to the south, bringing up the development of arts and crafts of the Southern Song Dynasty, particularly textile, printing and dyeing, shipbuilding, pottery, papermaking and printing. Besides, the overseas trade of the Southern Song Dynasty also developed rapidly, which also helped to promote the development of handicrafts.

During the period of the Song Dynasty and the Yuan Dynasty, the handicrafts of national minorities were affected by the culture and handicrafts of the Han nationality. They formed the handicraft production with their respective unique characteristics and obtained the achievements that attracted people's attention, such as the Liao Porcelain, the gold vessel and silverware of the Liao Dynasty, the Jun Porcelain of the Jin Dynasty, the celadon and underglaze red of the Yuan Dynasty, and the dying and weaving of the Xixia Dynasty and the Yuan Dynasty. After founding its state, the Liao Dynasty developed porcelain industry by setting up an official post specially taking care of kiln business, mainly copying the porcelain system of the Dingyao Kiln and its variety was typically represented by cockscomb pot resembling leather bag. In the later stage of the Jin Dynasty, new creation occurred in the respect of ceramic technology, particularly the Jun Porcelain initiating the decorative porcelain with red spots in cyan glaze. Of all the handicrafts in the Xixia Dynasty, fur handicraft was the most developed.

Lacquer plate with gardenia patterns by Zhang Cheng of the Yuan Dynasty.

The handicraft of the Yuan Dynasty suffered serious damage during its ceaseless expedition. However, the Yuan Dynasty paid great attention to recruit artisans from the prisoners of war to meet the needs in military affairs and daily life. Those artisans making weaponry were put in "military artisan" establishment while the artisans of other handicrafts were called "civil artisans." The status of artisans was hereditary, engaging in productive labor under surveillance.

Of all the handicrafts in the Yuan Dynasty, the achievement made in dyeing and weaving handicraft was the most important. A technique weaving gold filament in silk fabrics was the unique feature of the Yuan Dynasty, represented by a kind of brocade woven with gold filament in silk fabrics called "nashishi." It was woven mainly to meet the enjoyment of nobles but also for granting a reward. In this field, the technique of the artisans of the Hui nationality was the best. In the Yuan Dynasty, the technique of cotton weaving was also universally developed. Cotton fabrics, excellent in quality and reasonable in price, replaced traditional fabric of bast fibers and became very popular. Huang Daopo (c.1245-?) of Songjiang, Jiangsu (now under the jurisdiction of Shanghai), made great contributions to promoting the advanced technique of cotton spinning and weaving.

Rulers of the Yuan Dynasty were intrepid and valiant. In the nomadic life, their life style of eating and drinking with enthusiasm formed the style of straightforwardness, unconstraint, and sturdiness in the handicrafts of the Yuan Dynasty. Their thick and heavy, crude and large ceramic household utensils and splendid and impressive-looking silk fabrics were the typical expression of their style. The Yuan Dynasty also paid great attention to the dissemination of different religions, of which Buddhism and Taoism prevailed. In various kinds of handicrafts, religion was the subject frequently seen. The expansion of domain and development of traffic in the Yuan Dynasty made frequent the contacts among the various nationalities at home and the exchanges with other countries, which promoted the dissemination and development of industrial arts as well as the absorption and compromise of the styles of foreign lands.

# Arts and Crafts during the Ming and Qing Dynasties

The artisan system of the Ming Dynasty inherited the hereditary system of the Yuan Dynasty. Artisans had more personal freedom. During the non-service period, they had the freedom to be freely engaged in handicraft profession, which promoted the development of handicrafts.

The handicrafts of the Ming Dynasty achieved obvious development in both technology and art and many handicraft varieties formed their respective famous centers of production. Jingdezhen was the nationwide pottery-making center. During different periods there were different technological characteristics and various kinds of utensils, such as the *Yashou Bei* (a kind of cup) during the Yongle period (1403-1424), the celadon during the Xuande period (1426-1435), the colored celadon and the *Ji Gang Bei* (another kind of cup) during the period of Chenghua (1465-1487), the mono-colored glaze during the period of Zhengde (1506-1521), and the export-oriented porcelain during the period of Jiajing

Round-backed armchair from the Ming Dynasty, well-proportioned in scale and lofty in shape.

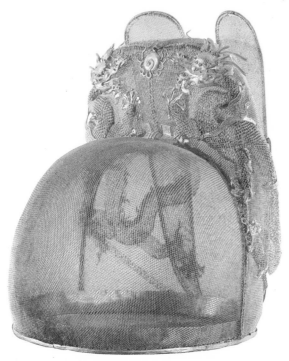

Gold crown from the Ming Dynasty, 24 cm high, woven with extremely thin gold filament, having two dragons vying with each other for a pearl on the top. It is one of the masterpieces of gold and silver handicrafts of Ming Dynasty.

(1522-1565) and Wanli (1573-1619). The technology of dyeing and weaving in the Ming Dynasty developed by leaps and bounds, such as the silk weaving in Suzhou and Hangzhou, the cotton weaving of Songjiang, the printing and dyeing of Wuhu, and the embroidery of the Gu School in Shanghai. The metal handicraft was featured with the *Xuande Lu* (a batch of small copperware cast with the copper mined in southeast Asia for meeting the demands of offering sacrifices to gods and ancestors as well as for lavendering clothes) and cloisonné (a kind of enamel with copper base and clipped copper wire). The development of garden buildings, the abundance of timber and the improvement of carpenter's tools brought up the developed furniture handicraft of the Ming Dynasty, which was known for its simple and unsophisticated shape, perfect handicrafts and refined style. In the Ming Dynasty, numerous craftsmen came to the fore, such as Gong Chun and Shi Dabin skilled in *Zisha Tao* (purple-clay pottery), Han Ximeng clever at the embroidery of the Gu School, Madame Ding skillful in cotton, Yang Xun accomplished in golden lacquer, Lu Zigang good at jade carving and the family of

Zhu are talented at bamboo carving.

In the Ming Dynasty, the new idealist philosophy "Knowledge is action" put forward by Wang Shouren was very popular. Meantime, a school of thought emphasizing erudition, another stressing practical purpose and still another accentuating scientific studies all came into being. In the later period of the Ming Dynasty, Wang Gen raised the assertion "For common people, practical use is the correct way," which promoted the emergence of monographs on arts and crafts. For instance, Huang Dacheng (a lacquer artisan of Xin'an, Anhui) and Ji Cheng (1579-?), a garden designer of Wujiang, Jiangsu, summed up their experiences and wrote the *Xiu Shi Lu* and the *Yuan Ye* (Garden Design) respectively. The *Tiangong Kaiwu*, written by Song Yingxing (1587-?) was praised as an "encyclopedia of arts and crafts in 17th century of China," which summed up in a scientific way the process of production and division of specialties of various kinds of handicrafts in the Ming Dynasty.

Zheng He went on his occidental voyages for seven times and expanded the economical and cultural exchanges between China and other countries. In the later period of the Ming Dynasty, the seeds of production relations of capitalism appeared in the regions south of the Yangtze River. The Western science and technology, such as machinery and physiology, were steadily introduced into China by missionaries. These factors promoted an all-around development of the industrial art of the Ming Dynasty and a handicraft style, refining, dignified, simple and decorative, was finally formed. Obviously the handicrafts of the Ming Dynasty formed two major systems: the court handicraft and folk handicraft. The former laid stress on technology and the means of expression was rigorous while the latter inclined to artistic expression and had a strong flavor of life. In a word, the handicraft of the Ming Dynasty was a matured period for the development of the national style of the industrial art of China, available basically with the main features of the modern times.

At the beginning of the Qing Dynasty, with the recovery of agriculture, handicrafts and commerce developed. During the reign of Kangxi (1662-1722), Yongzheng (1723-1735) and

Multicolored blue-and-white vase from the Qing Dynasty, collected in Musée Guimet, France.

Qianlong (1736-1795), ceramics, dyeing and weaving, lacquer ware, and carving and engraving all developed to some extent. In the respect of ceramics, Jingdezhen was still the porcelain-making center, developed in firing technology and various in glaze varieties. During the Kangxi Empire, priority was given to ancient colors, vigorous and robust; during the rule of Yongzheng, colored porcelain was the most outstanding, tasteful and delicate; and during the reign of Qianlong, enameled color porcelain was the greatest achievement, overelaborate and meticulous. In the respect of dyeing and weaving, the silk and satin of Suzhou and Hangzhou, the cloud brocade of Nanjing, the brocade of Sichuan, the textile of Guangdong, the printing and dyeing of Shanghai, the rug of Xinjiang and Ningxia were known

Painted enamel pot from the Qing Dynasty, collected in the Palace Museum.

Portable lacquer hand-warmer
with landscape patterns traced in
gold from the Qing Dynasty,
collected in the Palace Museum.

nationwide. Embroidery also formed local characteristics and respective technological systems with the embroidery of Suzhou, Guangdong, Sichuan, Hu'nan and Beijing as the most famous. Of the metal handicraft, cloisonné had somewhat innovation with the Qianlong period as the most developed. As all techniques were comprehensively used, it became a commodity for export at the end of the Qing Dynasty. Lacquer ware gradually formed different fabrication centers with respective local features, such as the carved lacquer ware of Beijing, the lacquer ware of Yangzhou inlaid with mother-of-pearl, and the bodiless lacquer ware of Fuzhou. The painted clay figurine of the Qing Dynasty was represented by the artisan "Clay Figurine Zhang" of Tianjin and the clay figurine of Huishan, Wuxi. They were either combined with practical use or used as toys, very popular among the people. In the respect of ornament, the auspicious patterns, popular in the Ming Dynasty and the Qing Dynasty, achieved the effect of "having meaning in all pictures and expressing auspiciousness in all implications" through the use of symbol, implication, homonym, metaphor, and Chinese character.

In short, the arts and crafts of the Qing Dynasty inherited the tradition of the Ming Dynasty and had some development in its production technology and artistic creation before its middle stage. The handicraft creation tended to be sophisticated and exquisite during the later stage but the production skills still had certain development. The varieties of the handicraft arts of the Qing Dynasty were plentiful and technological skills were applied in a comprehensive way, which can be used for our reference. However, the drawing-like ornament that played a leading role is neither in coordination with utensils nor with shapes, so it is inappropriate for us to use it in handicraft articles. Some handicraft varieties even applied foreign culture in a mechanical way for ornament. That is not what we should learn from. With the change of the modern social formation and people's way of life in China, the industrial art of China has undergone a transformation from traditional form to modern form and given first place to the life of the masses. As a result, machines are used for the main technology to make handicraft articles, which fits in with the modern aesthetic taste, concise and practical.

# Arts and Crafts in the Field of Utensil

# Ceramics

China is a world-renowned ancient country of ceramics, which has long been one of the most significant traditional handicrafts in China. As early as the early Neolithic Age 8,000 years ago, earthenware was already made and used. During the mid-Shang Dynasty, porcelain in its rudimentary form started to appear. In terms of crafts, pottery and porcelain are both silicate products made at different stage of development, porcelain being derived from pottery. They differ in raw materials, firing temperature and physical properties. Pottery was not phased out when porcelain invented, but continued to develop on its own course parallel to that of porcelain.

During the late Neolithic Age, painted pottery emerged as an outstanding variety of handiwork. And the then Neolithic Culture was called Painted Pottery Culture, also known as Yangshao Culture, named after Yangshao Village, Mianchi County, Henan Province where relics abound in pottery painted with colorful patterns were first found. Painted pottery is a kind of earthenware in reddish brown or pale brown with red or black decorative patterns elegant in shape and exquisite in design. Painted pottery was distributed over a vast area, including the Yangshao Culture

Painted earthen pot of the Majiayao Culture of the Neolithic Age, housed in the National Museum of China.

region in the upper and middle reaches of the Yellow River, the Dawenkou Culture region in the middle and lower reaches of the Yellow River (dating back to 4,500-6,400 years ago), and the Hemudu Culture region in the middle and lower reaches of the Yangtze River, of which Yangshao Culture was the most flourishing. Painted pottery was superior in ornamentation. As people at that time used to place utensils on the ground, the ornamental patterns tended to take an upper position while taking into consideration at the same time the vertical view and the side view so as to embody an integral effect.

As time goes by, painted pottery fell into decline, replaced by black pottery arising from the lower reaches of the Yellow River and the eastern coastal area. The Black Pottery Culture was also called Longshan Culture, as remains of this culture were first discovered in Longshan County, Licheng City, Shandong Province. By that time, black pottery had begun to be made by wheels which, as an innovation in process, made the shape of the pottery perfectly round and neat, the thickness of the body even, and productivity in making pottery raised. In the meantime, kiln sealing technique had been grasped, and the structure of the pottery kiln improved. The flame mouth was made smaller and the combustion chamber deeper so that the temperature of the kiln chamber became higher. Black pottery wares were jet-black in color, light in weight and bright on the surface. They were easy to string or to add ear-like handle. To make up for the blemish that as their dark appearance was hard to decorate, black pottery wares were often beautifully shaped.

Original porcelain appeared first in the Shang Dynasty, covered with dark green glaze slightly tinged with yellowish brown. The treatment of material was rough and preparation for the clay base crude. By the late Eastern Han Dynasty, porcelain production came to maturity. Specialized kilns for baking porcelain emerged in Zhejiang Province which became a center of celadon production. In the Six Dynasties Period, celadon became prevailing over a greater expanse of area.

By the late period of the Northern Dynasties, the successful development of white porcelain had opened a new era in the history of Chinese ceramics. During the Sui and Tang

Pierced black earthen cup with thin handle of the Longshan Culture, housed in Shandong Provincial Museum. The thin tube joining three parts of the cup keeps well formed after baking, indicating the superb skills in pottery making at that time.

Double-ear jug of the Geyao Kiln, housed in the Palace Museum.

*43*

dynasties, China saw an unprecedented booming in politics, economy, culture and commerce, which carried forward the progress of porcelain manufacturing, expanded the porcelain market and helped to form porcelain-making pattern of "celadon-in-the-south and white-porcelain-in-the-north," meaning that celadon was mainly manufactured in the southern part of the country, represented by the variety baked in the kiln of Yue, featuring light-and-thin shape, fine-and-close texture, and smooth-and-sleek to feel whereas white porcelain, represented by the kiln of Xing in the north, was characterized by sturdiness, compactness, snow-white in color and resonant as chime stone. Tang Tricolor, that is, the pottery artworks of the Tang Dynasty marked by its gorgeous color and rich varieties including household articles as well as funerary objects, was fabulous in the Tang Dynasty ceramics. By the end of the Tang Dynasty up to the Five Dynasties, famous kilns started to mushroom, making a new era in the history of Chinese ceramics.

The Song Dynasty was an age when well-known kilns came forth in large numbers, spreading all over the country to form gradually into six major schools including the Ding Kiln (in present-day Quyang, Hebei Province), Yaozhou Kiln (in Tongchuan, Shaanxi Province), Jun Kiln (in Yu County, Henan Province), Cizhou Kiln (in Ci County, Hebei Province), Longquan Celadon Kiln (in Longquan, Zhejiang Province) and Jingdezhen Kiln (in Jingdezhen, Jiangxi Province). The painted white porcelain baked in the above kilns each had their unique features: the Ding Porcelain meticulous in composition, Yao Celadon incisive and unconstrained, Jun Porcelain bright and gorgeous, Ci Porcelain rich in local flavor, Longquan Celadon luxuriantly verdant, Jingdezhen Porcelain crystal-clear. Altogether they opened a new sphere for the Chinese ceramics. Besides, in the Song Dynasty, porcelain dippers were widely used as teacups, among which, the black glazed ones were especially favored for a time.

The Chinese ceramic crafts entered a new stage of development during the Yuan, Ming and Qing dynasties. The mould-making became diversified, glaze was blazing with color and decorations were resplendent. The painted porcelain, then widely spread, was divided into two kinds:

Porcelain kiln of the Ming Dynasty, an illustration in *Tiangong Kaiwu* (Exploitation of the Works of Nature).

the overglaze porcelain and the underglaze porcelain. With overglaze porcelain the blanks are painted before coating with a transparent glaze and then fired at a temperature of 1,300 degrees centigrade. The overglaze porcelain usually has soft color that looks tasteful. Its color, under the protection of the glaze, tends to be wear-resisting and color-fast. However, as only a few coloring materials can stand high temperature, the overglaze porcelain is limited in varieties. The overglaze porcelain originated in the Tang Dynasty in the Changsha Kiln. From the Song and Yuan dynasties onwards, quite a number of new varieties appeared including the underglaze red, blue-and-white, etc. The overglaze porcelain is prepared by painting on glazed porcelain wares already fired in the kiln and then fired again in the kiln at a lower temperature. Such porcelain is rich in color, as much more coloring materials can be found that can stand the temperature required in the firing process. The blemish is that color is susceptible to friction or erosion by acid or alkaline, causing problems such like color fading and color change. The overglaze porcelain was initiated in the Ci Kiln in the Song Dynasty. By the Ming Dynasty, single-color overglaze and multi-color glaze techniques had already been fully developed. By the Qing Dynasty, more overglaze varieties were innovated, such as ancient color, enamel color and mixed color, etc.

Blue-and-white porcelain flat vase with dragon pattern of Ming Dynasty, housed in Palace Museum.

In the Yuan Dynasty the blue-and-white porcelain and the underglaze red porcelain each had distinguishing features. Jingdezhen, the porcelain capital, rose to prominence in the Yuan Dynasty, whose blue-and-white porcelain was the most typical of its products at that time. The blue-and-white porcelain is a kind of underglaze porcelain, using metal elements such as cobalt salt as coloring agent to paint blue flowers on a white background. As only one color is used and one firing needed, the process is simple and easy and is therefore extensively used in porcelain decoration. Besides, as the blue-and-white porcelain, like the blue-and-white printed cloth, has the artistic effect of being plain yet elegant, rich while unitary and changing with the color mixing and color gradation, was much favored by the broad masses of the people and soon became one of the principal varieties since the Yuan Dynasty. The blue-and-white decoration, which takes subject matters largely from traditional wash painting, appears bright and clean, extremely charming. Other subject matters for blue-and-white decoration include historic figures, tales and legends, taken from dramas and novels popular at that time. The underglaze red porcelain gets its name from the red color under the glaze. Its color glaze effect was formed naturally at first, but became an artificially decorated variety later on, as the gorgeous color and the warm atmosphere accorded with the traditional customs of the Chinese people. The blue-and-white underglaze red is commonly called "blue-and-white plus purple," characterized by patterns such like fruits and flowers painted amid the blue-and-white patterns. It was one of the outstanding representatives invented by Jingdezhen in the Yuan Dynasty, well-known for its magnificent colors, and has always been regarded as a rare variety of ancient Chinese porcelain, owing to the great degree of difficulty in baking.

Qing-dynasty multicolored flower-and-bird *zun* (wine vessel) from Jingdezhen, housed in Palace Museum.

In the Ming Dynasty, the porcelain craft achieved a breakthrough in that bamboo tools were replaced by potter's wheel in shaping blanks, and dip-glazing replaced by blow-glazing, and thus enhanced greatly the quality and quantity in porcelain manufacturing. With rapid progress in economy and transportation, a large number of imperial kilns and private kilns were established, which satisfied the need of the court, the daily use of ordinary households as well as exportation. From the Ming Dynasty onwards, white porcelain prevailed, which had opened a new field for porcelain decoration to develop. Jingdezhen at that time was still the center of porcelain making in the country, whereas celadon in Longquan of Zhejiang Province, white porcelain in Dehua of Fujian Province and purple-clay pottery in Yixing of Jiangsu Province were also known home and abroad. Among them the porcelain Buddha sculpture made of Dehua white porcelain was the most characteristic; the purple-clay pottery was known from its unique color, which excels in its

A pottery artisan.

outer appearance. The purple-clay teapots are always popular among people having a liking for tea.

During the Qing Dynasty glaze coloring increased in variety, such as red glaze in the Kangxi Period (1662-1722), jasper glaze and rouge water glaze in the Yongzheng Period (1723-1735), and multicolor glaze comprising red, blue, green, yellow and purple in the Qianlong Period (1736-1795). In color painting, ancient color, mixed color and enamel color painting achieved a higher level. Ancient color was a major variety in the Kangxi reign, which succeeded the multicolor technique of the Ming Dynasty, appearing gaudy, rich with distinct shades of color. Mixed glaze started in the Kangxi reign but well-developed in the Yongzheng reign, with a soft-and-elegant hue, and neat-and-meticulous drawing. By the middle period of Qing Dynasty, overseas coloring process started to be used when Western decorative techniques spread to China. Enamel coloring, the first imported coloring material also known as foreign coloring, was used in the Kangxi reign. In the Yongzheng reign, foreign coloring agents could already be manufactured at home. When it came to Qianlong period, the manufacturing of enamel coloring porcelain came up to the peak of development. The porcelain bodies were produced in Jingdezhen, transported to Peking where they were painted and fired for the second time. Enamel coloring porcelain is characterized by being glittering and transparent, and fine-grained, giving a sense of rising when used as ornament.

Apart from Jingdezhen as the center, porcelain production had almost spread to every corner of the country, with products sold not only at home, but exported to various countries in the world. It can be well said that the development of ceramics in the Ming and Qing dynasties has had a significant influence on Chinese ceramics today.

## Bronze Ware

The arising of bronze ware in China goes back to an early age. A bronze sword made by single mould 5,000 years ago unearthed at the site of Majiayao in Gansu Province, is to date the earliest bronze object discovered. For several thousand years, Chinese craftsmen have mastered superb techniques in bronze ware manufacturing to form unique style as regards the technological process, mould-making and decorative patterns.

During the late years of Neolithic Age, some archaeological culture had entered a time when both bronze and stone were used, which created prerequisite conditions for the development of bronze ware. The artistic factors of bronze ware can be traced in the stone artifacts, pottery and jade articles made in the late years of Neolithic Age. For example, shapes of bronze implements and weapons originated mostly from stone ware, whereas the shaping of bronze vessels was inherited from pottery mould-making. From bronze tripods, caldrons and goblets you can find their respective prototype. And such is the case with decorative patterns on bronze ware. Take the distinguished *taotie* (a rapacious animal in Chinese mythology) pattern, a common decorative pattern on ancient Chinese bronze ware, for an instance. Its source can be traced back to the jade articles in the Longshan Culture in the Neolithic Age. The Erlitou Culture that came between Longshan Culture and Shang Culture had already entered the Bronze Age. The bronze ware found in Erlitou, in addition to tools, weapons and articles for personal adornments, includes vessels made with double-mould and the noticeable turquoise-inlaid technique.

Rubbings of animal face pattern.

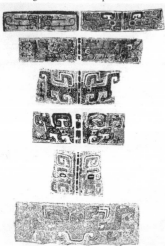

Natural copper is reddish in color, hence the name *hongtong* (red copper). Bronze is an alloy of copper and tin, a bit bluish in color, hence the name *qingtong* (blue copper). In a classic entitled *Powerful Nation*, Xun-tzu, the great master wrote, "moulds standard, materials fine, skills consummate, heat-control appropriate," which is just about the technology in bronze ware making. The process includes metal extracting from ore, mould making, casting and technical improvement. In the course of bronze manufacturing development, cold hammering was replaced by casting, and single mould replaced by double mould, which signifies a great leap forward in bronze technology. Mould making approach can be divided into two categories: the pottery mould approach and wax slip approach. By pottery mould approach two moulds, the inner and the outer are made with clay, the distance between the inner mould and the outer mould being the thickness of the body wall. By wax slip approach the body is made of wax which is covered with fine wet clay of a certain thickness, and then when the clay mould is dried, heat the wax till it is melted and flowed out of the mould, and then pours in melted bronze. The wax slip approach was initiated in the Spring and Autumn Period, and has been used ever since in making various complicated bronze wares.

Grand Simuwu quadripod of the late Shang Dynasty, housed in National Museum of China.

The book *Kao Gong Ji* (the Records of Examination of Craftsmen) states that the formula for compounding bronze contains six raw materials. That is the earliest explicit record in the world, giving the composition ratio of the alloy used in making bronze ware. Bronze ware has the advantage of low melting point and high hardness. Different bronze objects often have different ratios. For instance, in making bells or tripods, the proportion of copper to tin should be five to one, and in making axe, four to one. With such proportions bells and tripods can be bright in color, and axes tough and tensile.

The late years of Shang Dynasty reached the first height in the history of China's bronze ware development. The Yin Ruins of Anyang, Henan Province was the center of bronze

*Fifteen-Cupped Bronze Lamp* ( tree-shaped lamp) of Warring States Period, high 82.5 cm, base diameter 26 cm, stored in Cultural Relics Research Institute, Hebei Province.

ware production at that time. The early bronze articles were simply decorated, most single layered; later period objects were meticulously adorned with multi-layer figures featuring over-elaborate, rich and mysterious style. The decorative patterns on Yin and Zhou bronzeware for the most part are imaginary mythical animals, having an enigmatic, dignified atmosphere. This is owing to that the Shang people believed in ghosts and deities and that bronzeware was mainly used in offering sacrifices. The most commonly used design was *taotie*-pattern, characterized by a beast head with a straight bridge of the nose as center line to form symmetrical figure. *Taotie* figure was painted often on the major parts of the articles.

Often large-sized objects were cast in the Shang Dynsaty, of which the typical one is the celebrated *Simuwu Dafangding* (Grand Simuwu Quadripod). It is 133 centimeters in height, 78 centimeter in width, weighing 874 kilograms, the biggest bronzeware ever cast so far. On both sides beast face patterns and *kui* (a dragon-like monopode animal in ancient legends) figure are applied to adorn the edge, with other space unadorned so as to produce an artistic effect of contrast. On the whole the quadripod looks simple and powerful, dignified and magnificent. Standing in front of it a viewer is likely to feel stirring, to sense a force. The image of Grand Si Muwu Quadripod often appears as the symbol of ancient Chinese civilization. So heavy is the vessel that it has to be cast upside down, with the four legs upwards. The ears of the vessel are hollow, using joining-cast technique to cast. The work was done with at least two hundred craftsmen working in close cooperation, assisted by workers in charge of transport, burning charcoal, making a total of up to three hundred artisans. It is thus clear that the bronze technology at that time had achieved a high level capable of large-scale manufacturing.

During the Spring-and-Autumn Period up to the end of Warring-States Period, the application of bronzeware had shifted from offering sacrifices to daily household needs. Small objects for practical use were more and more favored by users. Practical functions had been added even to the original articles. Take the tripod made in the late years of the Spring and Autumn Period for an example. The three ring-ears on the lid enable the lid to be used as a plate when overturned. The subject matter for decoration gradually lost its mysterious atmosphere, the traditional animal design turned abstract, evolved into geometric figures, and more realistic themes reflecting social life such as feasting, hunting, war, etc. were added. The Square Pot with Lotus and Crane Design, with dragon-shaped ears, beast-shaped legs, a lid with two layers of lotus petals that spread outwards, in the middle of which stands a crane with wings spread as if ready

*Lotus-and-crane square pot* of Spring and Autumn Period, 118 cm high, 30.5 cm in diameter, housed in Palace Museum.

圖鼎鑄

Casting tripod, an illustration in *Tiangong Kaiwu* (Exploitation of the Works of Nature).

Suanni (legendary beast of prey) square mirror with grape patterns, side length 17.1 cm, housed in Shosoin Repository ( し ょうそういん), Nara (なら), Japan.

for flight, had created a new fashion of the day, which is pure, fresh and magnificent. The Fifteen-Cupped Bronze Lamp unearthed in the Zhongshan State (now the mid-eastern part of Hebei Province) in the Warring States Period, has tree trunk as lamp pole installed with fifteen small cups, with several monkeys in different shapes set here and there on the trunk, looking undeniably vivid.

During the Period of Spring-and-Autumn and Warring-States, bronzeware manufacturing came up to the highest level in history. Not only were separate-casting method and wax-slip method invented, but also new crafts and new techniques were adopted such as weld, inlay, etc., making bronzeware more rich and colorful. In particular in the late years of the Warring States Period, the use of sharp iron tools had caused the ornaments on bronzeware to develope from engraving designs to scratching designs by which means a line can be as thin as a hair. By applying the technique of gold and silver inlaying, copper, gold and silver wire, or gold and silver slices can be inlaid in the pattern intaglio to form various delicate and resplendent patterns. The Yanyue Yulie Gongzhan Hu (flask with designs of banquet and music, fishing and hunting, attacking and fighting), excavated at Baihuatan in Chengdu in 1965, is a representative work of gold-inlay technique. Using belt division method to display various scenes such as mulberry picking, shooting, hunting, feting, music playing, attacking and defending, and dividing each layer of designs with consecutive triangle cirrus patterns, the whole composition is made varying yet unitary. Since the Warring States Period, with the development of iron smelting technique, improvement of ceramic technology, and the rising of lacquer ware making, bronzeware gradually faded out of the mainstream stage of traditional Chinese technology.

Although bronzeware manufacture declined little by little, bronze mirror as a unique variety of bronze technology, continued its development for several hundred years more. The bronze mirror is used in dressing and making up. It is also used for monster-revealing and warding off evil spirits. Its manufacturing technology had experienced several more booming periods. From the Warring States Period, Han Dynasty, Tang Dynasty down to the Song Dynasty, mirrors were meticulously made, which look rich in style and highly decorative. In the Tang Dynasty a prevailing practice has been formed that bronze mirror was used as gift. According to *The Book of Tang: Records of Ritual and Music,* in the prosperous period of the Tang Dynasty, the birthday of Emperor Xuanzong, which falls on the fifth day of the eighth lunar month was stipulated as Eternity Day, on which officials must dedicate birthday wine and mirrors were used to congratulate the emperor's birthday. Such a practice had facilitated the development of bronze mirror, making it to form a requisitely ornamental and colorful style. The ornamental patterns used on mirrors comprise the four-deity pattern, twelve zodiac signs pattern, auspicious beast pattern, flower and bird pattern, figure pattern and Eight Trigrams pattern, all vivacious and lifelike.

Among the bronze horses unearthed in Wuwei of Gansu Province in 1969, the one named Steed Treading on Flying Swallow is the most outstanding. It shows a steed galloping ahead holding its head high, tail throwing up, three feet rising into the air, the right hind leg stepping on a flying swallow, which is extraordinary imaginative. The bronze lamps in the Han Dynasty were varied in style, all exquisitely made and in conformity with scientific principles, among which the most distinguished is the Changxin Palace Lamp excavated at Mancheng of Hebei Province, the pattern being a maid in an imperial palace in a half-kneeling, half-sitting posture, the left hand holding a lamp, the right hand carrying the lampshade, a sleeve serving as a siphon, forcing oil to flow

*Bronze galloping steed,* also known as steed stepping on the flying swallow, of Eastern Han Dynasty, 34.5 cm high, 45 cm long, housed in Palace Museum.

into the lamp body. The round lamp body has two tile-shaped movable shades, which can be used to regulate the direction of light. The ingenious design and exquisite technology fully manifest the combination of practical use and good taste.

# Lacquer

Lacquer ware is a sort of artefacts using wood or other materials as body on which lacquer is coated. Chinese lacquer has a long history. To date the oldest piece found is a lacquer-painted wooden bowl discovered in the Hemudu remains in Yuyao, Zhejiang Province in 1978, which went back 7,000 years.

In the Neolithic Age, lacquer was still at an exploring stage. From the Xia, Shang, and Western Zhou dynasties down to the Spring and Autumn Period, lacquer ware had experienced its initial prosperous period. During the Warring States Period and Han Dynasty, tree cultivation started to be taken seriously, conducive to lacquer production on a grand scale which lasted for centuries. *The classic Historical Records* writes that Chuang-tzu (c. 369-286 B.C.), the great philosopher was once an officer in charge of lacquer affairs. In the Han Dynasty, special administration was established to take charge of lacquer production, which was managed under

Vermillion wooden bowl of Hemudu Culture housed in Zhejiang Museum. It is the earliest lacquer ware discovered so far, coated with a thin layer of natural vermillion lacquer on the surface, slightly lustrous.

Painted lacquer inner coffin made in early Warring States Period, unearthed from Zenghouyi tomb in Suizhou, Hubei, kept in Hubei Museum.

strict organization with elaborate division of labor. The inscriptions on Han Dynasty lacquer utensils excavated in Rakrang of Korea in 1932 tell in detail the date, location, division of work and names of officials involved in the manufacturing. According to the records, division of labor was clear and definite, in which lacquer body preparing, lacquer coating, painting, bronze buckle fixing, finishing, etc., each was done by specific craftsmen. In addition, there were workers specialized in making lacquer, providing materials, etc.

In the early Warring States Period, lacquer ware body was made of wood, which is thick and heavy. Later on, other materials were adopted such as the lightweight wood-chips, composite materials (gray ash generated from the sumac reinforced with flax fibers), tough oxhide, etc. The State of Chu was the hub of lacquer production at that time where the articles made were red and black in color, mostly red patterns painted on black background with primitive simplicity. Animal patterns, geometric figures, and patterns reflecting social life such as chariot and horses, dancing, hunting, etc. were used for decoration. Already were products rich in variety, to be used not only as utensils, stationery, ornaments for furniture, but also for musical instruments, weapons and funerary objects, partly in place of bronzeware. They were therefore much favored by dukes and princes in spite of their high price.

On the basis of the Warring States Period, lacquer craft attained new progress

Double-layer lacquer case of Western Han Dynasty, unearthed from Han tombs at Mawangdui, Changsha. It contains nine smaller cases different in size and shape for various uses.

in the Han Dynasty, production scale expanded and production area more extensive, centered on the Shu and the Guanghan prefectures of Sichuan Province. The cloud-patterned lacquer bell 57 centimeters high and the cloud-and-dragon patterned lacquer plate 53.6 centimeters in diameter are typical large-sized lightweight artifacts reflecting the advancement of the art of lacquer. Full set of lacquer works had appeared, such as multi- latticed cassette which contains as many as nine, even eleven lattices different in size and shape, which are both practical and space-saving. The prevailing ornamental patterns included floating-cloud patterns and animal patterns, which are rich in color, with lines vigorous and racy, drawing vivacious and spirit resonant.

When it came to the Eastern Han Dynasty, lacquer manufacture entered a period of slow progress, though not without some noteworthy results. In the Tang Dynasty, the gold and silver peace level-off craft was a marked achievement. The process is first to have thin silver and gold sheets made in the shape of characters, birds, animals, flowers, etc. affixed to smoothed lacquer body, and then apply two or three layers of lacquer on the body when it is dried, then grind the body till the golden and silvery patterns appeared. Finally polish to make a finished product. Lacquer articles made under such technique, though costly and time-

Lacquer box with cloud pattern of Yuan Dynasty, housed in Anhui Museum, a representative work of Zhang Cheng, master of lacquer making.

consuming, are highly refined, with golden and silvers luster pleasing to the eye. It is recorded in the ancient books *Miscellaneous Notes of Youyang* and *Deeds of An Lushan* that Emperor Xuanzong of the Tang Dynasty and his concubine Yang Yuhuan had bestowed to his patronized official An Lushan lacquer articles manufactured using the above-said craft. In the Song Dynasty the gold inlay craft was initiated, the process of which is to carve patterns on the surface of the lacquer and then fill gold powder into the intaglio. At that time, lacquer ware was produced not only by the government, but by ordinary people. In the masterpiece painting *Pure Brightness Day on the River*, one can detect private-run lacquer store in Kaifeng, then the capital of Northern Song Dynasty.

Tang-dynasty bronze mirror with silver peace background, housed in the National Museum of China.

During Yuan, Ming and Qing dynasties, a new upsurge in lacquer ware production arose. Governmental and non-governmental undertakings coexisted and co-developed. The carving paint technology had achieved brilliant results in which fluid and smooth patterns were formed on thickly spread lacquer using a special cutting skill by a bunch of outstanding craftsmen. In the Ming and Qing dynasties, the lacquer technology, combined with architecture and furnishings, turned from the sphere of practical use towards adornment, producing

some four hundred varieties under fourteen major categories including overspreading, tracing design in gold, carving-inlay, etc.

During the Yongle Period (1403-1424) of Ming Dynasty, a lacquer-making institution serving the royal court exclusively called Guoyuanchang was established in which two kinds of lacquer, the carving paint lacquer and the inlaying lacquer were exquisitely produced, known as royal production. In the meantime, production among the common people was also popular with a host of outstanding craftsmen revealed, such as Jiang Huihui from Suzhou, a dab at gold-lacquer, Yang Xun who went to Japan to learn Japanese lacquer technology, and Zhou Zhu who was skilled in the "hundred-treasure inlay" technique. Moreover, in the Ming Dynasty, the sole extant ancient book about lacquer technology – *Lacquering* was written by Huang Dacheng, a master artisan in lacquer work from Xin'an (present-day Xin'an County, Anhui Province). In giving an account in detail of lacquer making procedures, materials, implements, color lacquer formula, decoration methods, etc., it well inherited, summarized, and developed China's lacquer technology.

Based on the achievements of Ming Dynasty lacquer work, a number of manufacturing hubs appeared in the Qing Dynasty, each specialized in an individual species with local flavor, such as carving lacquer in Beijing, mother-of-pearl inlay lacquer in Yangzhou, bodiless lacquer in Fujian, etc. Tom Chippendale, famous British furniture maker in the 18th century, ever designed lacquer furniture using Chinese works for reference. The works he designed, adorned with patterns tinged with oriental appeal such as dragon, flowers, Buddha, pagoda, etc., prevailed for a time known as "Times of Chippendale." The art of Chinese lacquer, as one of the significant varieties of Chinese traditional handicrafts, spread first to East Asia, Southeastern Asia, and then to North America via Western Europe and was well received there.

Vermilion bodiless lacquer tray of Qing Dynasty, housed in Palace Museum. It is only about half a millimeter in thickness, with a hue of red coral.

# Arts and Crafts in the Field of Apparel

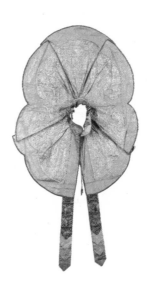

# Embroidery

Embroidery in China goes back to ancient times. Some four thousand years ago when China was passing from primitive society to slave society, there was a rule that the tribal leaders should wear formal attire with patterns of the sun, the moon, and stars embroidered on the upper garment; of weeds, fire, etc., on trousers (skirts) when grand ceremonies were held such as celebrations, sacrifice-offerings, etc..

In the Spring and Autumn and the Warring States Period, along with the progress of agriculture, the lifestyle that men plough the fields and women weave became more firmly fixed, mulberry-and-hemp planting and spinning-and-weaving extensively spread, and the embroidery craft grew mature gradually. To date the earliest embroidery works handed down from ancient times are the two pieces unearthed from the Chu Tombs in the Warring States Period. By applying braid embroidering method (also known as locking embroidering) that features neat stitch, flowing line, and tasteful coloring, the patterns of swimming-dragon and dancing-phoenix; fierce-tiger and auspicious-beast embroidered on silks appear natural and lifelike, which gives full expression to the achievements of embroidery art in the ancient State of Chu.

When it came to Qin and Han dynasties, the art of embroidery further developed following the progress of silk-spinning. A diversified batch of embroidered works well preserved was unearthed from the Han tombs at Mawangdui of Changsha, Hu'nan Province. These embroideries, which represent the artistic style as well as the high level of embroidery in the Han Dynasty, mostly have patterns of ripple-like clouds, soaring phoenix, galloping holy beasts, ribbon-shaped flowers, geometric figures, etc., using basically locking method with neat stitching, compact composition and smooth lines.

The prevailing practice of embroidering Buddha started from the last years of Han Dynasty. During the Six Dynasties, foreign culture represented by Buddhism mingled with local culture, which reflected in embroidery. Some silk fragments unearthed from the Eastern Jin Dynasty down to the Northern Dynasties unearthed in Dunhuang of Gansu Province, and Hetian, Bachu, Turpan of Xinjiang Uygur Autonomous Region, reveal that the whole piece of work, design and blank in all, was fine and closely embroidered using locking technique, producing the effect of covering the fabrics to the full with embroidery. In the book entitled *Famous Paintings through the Ages*, Zhang Yanyuan, a Tang Dynasty writer writes that Lady Zhao in the court of the State of Wu was distinguished for her "three matchlessness" – matchlessness in weaving, in stitching and in silk. She was adept at weaving dragon and phoenix patterned brocade with colorful silk thread, called "matchlessness of weaving;" embroidering the Five Holy Mountains on a square piece of fabric, "called matchlessness of stitching;" and making soft curtains with a specific kind of silk named Jiaoshu silk, called "matchlessness of silk." Another notable feature of embroidery at that time is that human figures had started to appear on embroidered works.

Although the Han-Dynasty locking embroidery technique was still followed in the Tang Dynasty, another skill called plain stitching method had already been widely used together with some other stitching methods, using color thread and wider range of fabrics. Besides, patterns were edged with golden and silvery thread to give a three-dimensional effect. During the Tang and Song dynasties, as more and more people joined in embroidery, the representative needlework among females – boudoir embroidery, emerged. At the same time, as scholar-painters widely took part in the work, there appeared embroidery painting, which combines painting with embroidery, with designs contributed by painters and embroidery made by artisans. From Tang down to Ming and Qing dynasties, the participation of scholar-painters in the business had carried forward the innovation and development of embroidery techniques: in the treatment of

*Flowery Brook – Fisher's Retreat*: Ming-dynasty Gu-embroidered painting, 33.4 cm vertical, 24.5 cm horizontal, collected in Palace Museum.

Qing-dynasty Gu-embroidered picture album *West Lake*, 24.1 cm high, 26.3 cm wide, housed in Taipei Palace Museum. The picture shows the scene of "*Orioles Singing in the Willows.*"

Qing-dynasty Suzhou embroidered cuff edge with 12 Chinese zodiac signs patterns (partial), housed in Suzhou Embroidery Research Institute.

color silk , thread was cut into finer bits, so that the lines might appear more soft and graceful; in stitching methods, there appeared various new approaches, such as arbitrary stitching, thread nailing, gold circling, mixing stitching, rolling stitching, and linking stitching.

In the Ming and Qing dynasties, the government-run handicraft business waned gradually. Non-governmental workshops started to arise, thus facilitating the growth of folk handicrafts. Thanks to the cooperation between scholars and artisans, embroidery skills and production became brisk and thriving. Traditional Chinese embroidery reached its summit of prosperity, with four famous schools of embroidery:

Su-embroidery, Yue-embroidery, Shu-embroidery and Xiang-embroidery coming into being.

Centering on the city of Suzhou, Su-embroidery was developed on the basis of Gu-embroidery. Originally Gu-embroidery referred to the works done by the Gu family of Shanghai in the Ming Dynasty. Han Ximeng, wife to Gu Shouqian of the Gu family, was skilled at painting flowers and plants and in particular at embroidery, making the fame of Gu-family embroidery spread far and wide. In the Qing Dynasty, embroidery shops in the region south of the Yangtze River often hang up the sign "Gu-embroidery" to solicit customers. Su-embroidery, having extensively drawn the strong points of the Gu-embroidery, created its own varieties including the painting-imitation embroidery and portrait embroidery. Su-embroidery features that the landscape on the embroidery can depict the difference between the background and the distant view, the buildings appear deep and imposing, the figure looks vivid and the flowers and birds lifelike. In technology, overlapping stitching is mainly used, in which floss and thread overlapping without revealing any trace of stitching. Often three or four different kinds of thread either of the same color or of similar shade are applied to produce a hazy effect.

Yue-embroidery, being the general name for the embroidery in the Guangdong Province, is believed to be initiated by the Li people (a minority nationality). The embroidery workers in former times were mostly males from Guangzhou and Chaozhou. Their embroidered works

Qing-dynasty Guangdong embroidered card folder, 24 cm vertical, 39 cm horizontal, housed in Palace Museum.

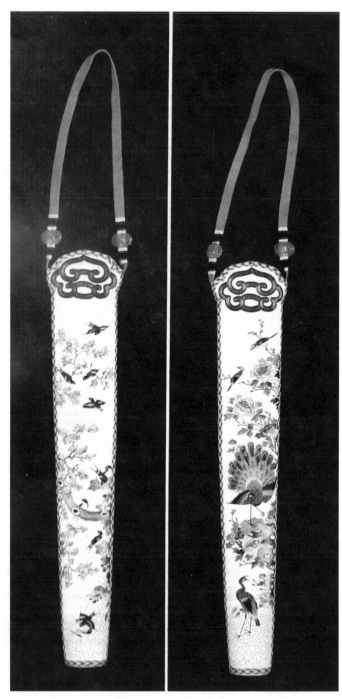

Qing-dynasty Guangdong embroidered fan kit housed in Palace Museum. On white satin background, apricot grove and swallow are embroidered on one side and peacock and peony on the other.

included primarily dress and adornments, hanging screens, shoulder bags, pictures on the screen, round fans, fan cases, etc. Currently subject matters of Yue-embroidery often involve phoenix, peony, pine and crane, deer, chicken and goose. The composition is usually elaborate and vital, coloring magnificent and dazzling, stitching simple and concise. Rough and loose thread is used to make uneven stitches, some longer and some shorter, overlapping one another and raised a bit. The gold-nailing embroidery is one of its quality varieties, the process of which is using satin background knitted with golden thread or nailed with golden floss, covered with loose golden floss design so that it looks resplendent. Works made using gold-nailing technique include stage costumes, furnishings for theaters and temples to heighten a warm and animated atmosphere.

Shu-embroidery, also known as Sichuan embroidery, is an age-old local craft based on Chengdu of Sichuan Province. According to the book *History of the State of Huayang* written by Chang Qu of Qin Dynasty, Shu-embroidery and Shu-brocade were two specialties of Sichuan Province. Shu-embroidery works mainly include quilt covers, pillow cases, garments, shoes and painted screens, mostly articles of everyday use. The designs are largely flowers, birds, insects, fish, folk auspicious words and traditional patterns, possessing jubilant flavor. Since the middle and later period of Qing Dynasty, on the basis of traditional local embroidery technique, Shu-embroidery took in the strong points in Gu-embroidery and Su-embroidery and sprang up overnight to become one of most important commodity embroidery varieties in the country. Shu-embroidery features neat stitching, smoothness and brightness, with lines clear, color gorgeous, pattern-edge uniform as if cut with knife.

Xiang-embroidery is the general name of embroidered works made in Hu'nan Province, Changsha being a hub. At first merchants in Changsha set up the "Gu-embroidery Shop" to cater for the newly appointed high official who rose to power by suppressing the Taiping Revolution. Soon it had prevailed over Gu-embroidery.

Qing-dynasty Li nationality embroidered dragon quilt. On background woven from rough kapok thread is 63 cm long patterns of phoenixes and Chinese unicon.

65

Xiang-embroidery is characterized by using silk floss to embroider flowers. The silk floss is treated in a certain solution so as to prevent pills from appearing. Xiang-embroidery is called "fine wool embroidery" by local people. Using traditional painting as subject matter, Xiang-embroidery boasts vivid and lifelike shape and unconstrained style, well commended as "flowers embroidered seemingly fragrant, birds embroidered seemingly chirping, tigers embroidered seemingly running and figures embroidered seemingly true to life."

## Printing and Dyeing

Dyeing textiles using minerals and plants is a time-honored practice in China. Early in the Neolithic Age some six to seven thousand years ago, the Chinese ancients could already dye red sackcloth with hematite powder. Through long-term practice in production, Chinese people had learnt the techniques of dye-extracting and application to yield colorful fabrics.

During the Shang and Zhou dynasties, with dyeing techniques gradually improved, governmental officials were appointed such as "dyeing men," "dyestuff keepers," etc. in charge of relative affairs. In the ancient classic *The Book of Songs*, fabrics in various colors are mentioned, indicating that dyestuffs at that time were continuously increasing in varieties.

Eastern Han-dynasty blue-and-white flowery calico, 86 cm long, 45 cm wide, housed in Xinjiang Uygur Autonomous Region Museum.

The dyeing techniques came up to a rather high level in the Han Dynasty. There were two major approaches: weaving before dyeing, as with *juan*-silk, silk gauze and damask, and dying before weaving, as involving brocade. The brocades bearing the Chinese characters "*yan nian yi shou*" (meaning prolonging life) and "*wan shi ru yi*" (meaning everything going the way as one wishes) excavated from the Eastern Han tombs in Minfeng of Xinjiang Uygur Autonomous Region in 1959 were weaved with silk threads of diverse colors including crimson, white, yellow, brown, sapphire blue, pale blue, glossy dark green, dark reddish purple, pale orange, light tan, etc., manifesting the craftspeople's superb skills in dyeing and color matching. The Tang Dynasty silk fabrics unearthed in Turpan of Xinjiang are bright with as many as twenty four colors. Quite a few assorted colors were obtained by first dyeing primary colors and then applying process-dying method.

Batik works of Bai nationality in Dali, Yunnan Province.

The earliest printed fabric still in existence is the silk quilt cover buried in a Chu tomb in the Warring States Period. It was unearthed in Changsha of Hu'nan Province. Other pieces were discovered in the Western Han tombs in both Mawangdui of Changsha and Mozuizi of Wuwei, in Gansu Province. Among them was a piece of silk gauze with cloud patterns printed in golden and silvery colors against a grey background. It was process-printed using relief printing plates, rather advanced in crafts. It is strange such techniques had never been applied again in the several hundred years after the Western Han Dynasty. In the Central Plains, the revival of printing techniques started from *xie* (meaning valerian, here referring wax-valerian craft). Later on *xie* is used as a general name for printed fabrics. When it came to the Tang Dynasty, printing and dyeing crafts became highly developed. Wax-valerian, tie-dye and clip knot are regarded as three major printing processes in ancient China.

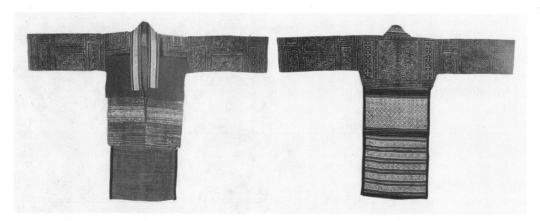

Qing-dynasty batik embroidered dress of Miao nationality, view of front and back.

Qing-dynasty batik lace of Bouyi nationality, manual woven by Guizhou Bouyi ethnic people and printed using traditional handicrafts.

Wax-valerian is also known as wax dyeing. Actually it is a wax-insulating dyeing method (batik). With this approach, patterns are drawn with wax on natural fiber fabrics such as hemp, silk, cotton, wool, etc. before dyeing. The wax prevents dyeing solution from entering the patterns. And then after heating to boil, wax is removed and patterns emerge. The condensation and contraction of the liquid wax causes cracks to appear on the patterns, forming unique natural veins. Wax dyeing as an age-old dye-insulating technique, can be traced back to as early as the Qin and Han dynasties when the ancestors of minority nationalities such as Miao, Yao, and Bouyi had already had a good command of the wax-dyeing process.

Tie-dyeing also known as ligation-dyeing is an ancient folk printing-dyeing process of binding fabrics before dyeing. The process is to sew the fabric with needle and threads into a certain shape, or bind the fabric tightly with thread in the light of the designs so that the fabric become crumpled and overlapping. As the crumpled part is hardly to be dyed whereas unbound part is easy to get dyed, a hazy effect will be produced. In the Jin Dynasty, tie-dyeing started to spread among the folk people. During the Southern and Northern Dynasties, there emerged designs such like the "Purple valerian foetus," well received for a while. By the Sui and

Tang dynasties, tie-dyeing became all the rage. Currently the earliest ancient tie-dyeing fabric we can see is the Jin Dynasty *juan*-silk unearthed from the Astana tomb in Xinjiang on which pinprick and crumple are still dimly visible.

Clip-knot was in vogue in the prosperous period of Tang Dynasty. The process is to put the fabrics between twin pieces of wooden board and then dye. Using this method the designs appear symmetric and balanced. At that time, clip-knot often applies to women's dress and adornments, sometimes as ornaments for furniture such as clip-knot screens, etc.

Valerian clip-knot *juan*-silk with hunting patterns of Tang Dynasty, 43.5 cm long, 31.3 cm long, stored in Xinjiang Uygur Autonomous Region Museum.

## Silk Weaving

The Chinese silk weaving is well known in the world for its long history, advanced crafts and fine workmanship. Silk fabrics in ancient times include the following varieties: *juan* (thin, tough silk), *sha* (gauze as a general term), *qi* (damask), *luo* (silk gauze), *jin* (brocade), *duan* (satin), *kesi* (brocade woven using a special craft).

In the Shang Dynasty, silk fabric with conspicuous twisting warp weave had already emerged. When it came to the Western Zhou Dynasty, more complicated brocade-weaving craft was developed. Down to the Spring and Autumn and Warring States Period, silk-weaving had attained a rather high level. Silk fabrics cover *juan, luo, sha,* and *jin*; the designs include rhombus pattern, S-shape pattern, and geometric patterns adorned with dragon, phoenix, human figure, etc. Silk weaving and knitting in the Qin and Han dynasties, Han in particular, made a leap forward on the basis of the Warring States Period tradition, containing more varied silk fabrics such as *jin, ling* (twill-weave silk), *qi, luo, sha, juan, gao* (thin and white silk), *wan* (fine silk fabrics), etc. The common designs on silk fabrics in the Han Dynasty include floating clouds, animals, flowers and plants, auspicious characters, and all sorts of geometric figures. The art of silk-weaving in the Han Dynasty was already elaborate, in

Monk's plain-gauze robe unearthed from Han-tombs at Mawangdui, Changsha, Hu'nan Province. It is made of highly fine natural silk, manifesting that Chinese silk weaving was already elaborate in workmanship at that time.

particular in the weaving of single-thread gauze with even distributed meshes, of which the representative work is a plain gauzed Buddhist monk's robe unearthed from the Han Tomb No.1 of Mawangdui in Changsha, Hu'nan Province. It measures 128 centimeters across from one end to the other end of the two sleeves, 190 centimeters long and yet weighs only 49 grams. Extremely marvelous!

Silk weaving in the Tang Dynasty was meticulous in the division of work. The Weaving and Dyeing Administration under the central government had been set up to take charge of production, while private silk-weaving businesses could be found all over the country, producing large quantity of fabrics. Craftspeople at that time did their utmost to seek gorgeous coloring effect. Among the multiple varieties, brocade was the best-known, called "Tang brocade." As is different from traditional craft in which warp was used to weave decorative patterns, Tang brocade-weaving, affected by the Western Region textile culture, used weft to form decorative patterns sandwiched between warp weave. It was called "weft brocade." The loom used for weft brocade by which decorative patterns are formed with multi-layer and multi-colored weft, is complicated in structure but easy to handle, capable of weaving more complex designs and broad fabrics. Since the middle period of Tang Dynasty, using weft to form decorative patterns had become the mainstream in silk jacquard weave. The Tang brocade, which assimilated exotic ornamental patterns, manifested a fresh, resplendent and imposing style. Aside from Tang brocade, *ling* (silk fabric with twill weave as basic characteristic) was also very popular, in particular the *liao-ling* manufactured in Zhejiang Province, which was best known at that time. Dou Shilun, best reputed silk pattern designer, usually took subject matters like sheep, horse, dragon, phoenix, etc. for decorative patterns. As what he designed often appear original, unconventional, and full of vitality, they were called "Duke of Lingyang patterns," as he was ever made Duke of Lingyang by the emperor.

The Song Dynasty silk weaving made further progress, in particular in the field of brocade, called "Song brocade." Using three kinds of twill weave, two kinds of warp (raw silk for the surface and colored boiled-off silk for the base) and three kinds of colored weft, the weave looks regular and neat, shades of color elegant and harmonious with small ornamental patterns. The Song brocade was used for dress and adornment, for reward and trade, and as a material for mounting pictures. At that time, *kesi* brocade was also very popular, used mainly for weaving works of art such as paintings and calligraphic works. It shows that the function

Work of Shen Zifan, *kesi* silk weaving craftsman of Southern Song Dynasty, meticulously depicting the serene and realistic style of flower-and-bird painting of Southern Song Dynasty.

Kesi silk-weaving: scroll flower-and-bird painting by Shen Zifan (partial).

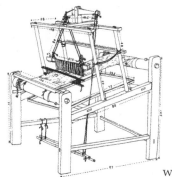

Kesi-weaving loom in Wuxian County, Jiangsu Province.

of silk-weaving crafts had been shifted from practical use to appreciation.

*Kesi* silk was produced in Dingzhou, Hebei Province in the Northern Song Dynasty, and around Yunjian (now Songjiang of Shanghai) area in the Southern Song Dynasty.

Between the Song and Yuan dynasties, a giant spinning wheel with several dozen spindles was invented on the basis of traditional wheels. The wheel, driven with waterpower and able to adapt to large-scaled production, already had the rudimentary form of modern spinning machinery. Take hemp spinning for an instance. An ordinary wheel could produce at most 1.5 kilograms of yarn a day, whereas the giant wheel could make over 50 kilograms in twenty four hours. It is a significant invention in ancient China using natural forces for textile machinery.

Gold-weaving was unique in silk weaving art in the Yuan Dynasty. The Yuan Dynasty rulers had partiality for gold, making gold weaving a fashion. The designs on golden brocade included dragon, phoenix, flower, tortoise shell,

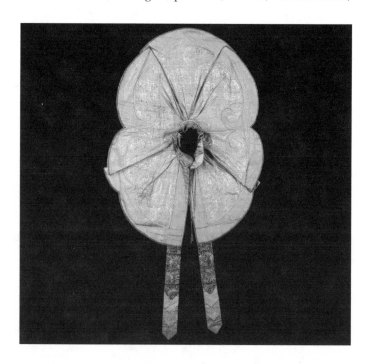

Yuan-dynasty golden thread damask cape, housed in Palace Museum.

*hui*-figure (a figure in the shape of the Chinese character *hui*), etc. In order to suit the needs of the nomadic Mongolian nationality, wool weaving got an opportunity to develop. The woven woolen articles were mostly carpets, bed mattress, saddles, shoes and headgear, produced mainly in Ningxia and Helin (now under Mongolian jurisdiction). In ancient China, cotton was planted only in northwest and southwest areas. Due to the work of Huang Daopo, a remarkable innovator of cotton textile crafts in the Yuan Dynasty who was a native of Wunijing, Songjiang (now in Shanghai), cotton textile spread far and wide. For a time, the "Wunijing quilt" became well-known in the whole country.

During the Ming Dynasty, there appeared four silk fabric producing areas: Shanxi, Sichuan, Fujian-Guangxi and the region south of the Yangtze River. At that time, brocade was

*Silk-reeling*, an illustration in *Tiangong Kaiwu* (Exploitation of the Works of Nature).

the kind of silk fabric embodying the most salient features of the times, called "Ming brocad." It is divided into three main categories: the warehouse brocade, golden-silvery brocade and flowery brocade. The warehouse brocade features grey coloring which appears soft and elegant. The golden-silvery brocade looks refined and glittering, with golden or silvery thread used for weaving. The flowery brocade is a jacquard fabric, using a special shuttle-moving process to insert colored silk threads in which every single flower is woven with different colors. Its multiple colors and large-sized flowers produce an effect of brilliance and magnificence. The flowery

New Year picture: *Spinning and Weaving*, a scene of nine Qing-dynasty women at work-cotton fluffing, spinning, yarn starching or weaving respectively.

brocade which first appeared during the Tang Dynasty and prevailed in the Ming and Qing dynasties represented the highest level of ancient Chinese silk weaving. The Ming brocade can be divided into light gauze, silk gauze, satin, and etc, according to their different base-fabrics. It is rich in patterns, such as clouds, dragon, phoenix, crane, flowers, plants, birds, butterfly, and propitious figures, all looking in good taste and full of stylized decorative beauty.

Three major silk-weaving centers were formed in Suzhou, Nanjing and Hangzhou in the Qing Dynasty, well-known for their rich varieties and exquisite workmanship. The artistic style at that time could largely be classified as the early stage, the middle stage and the late stage. At the early stage, the traditional features of the Ming Dynasty were inherited in which geometric figures were used as framework, embellished with small flowers. At the middle stage, as having been obviously influenced by the art styles of baroque and rococo from Europe, designs became complicated and gorgeous. At the late stage broken-sprig and large flower patterns were in fashion, tending to be simple, free and easy. Besides Yunnan brocade, Song-style brocade and Sichuan brocade, famous fabrics also include ancient fragrance satin and brocade satin in the Qing Dynasty. Satin is a shiny and smooth fabric appeared first in the Yuan Dynasty and became a mainstream silk fabric during the Ming and Qing dynasties.

# Arts and Crafts in the Field of Furnishings

# Furniture

Furniture is closely related to people's life-style and environment. The sitting posture of the Chinese people has changed from sitting on the floor as in ancient times to sitting on a seat as in present day. The shape of furniture falls accordingly into two series, the low-type and the high-type to suit people's needs at respective historical stages.

From the Shang and Zhou down to the Han and Wei dynasties, people used to sit on the floor or take a half-kneeling, half-sitting position. The limited pieces of furniture available at that time such as narrow oblong tables and side tables were all low and short, which could be moved about without being placed in fixed position. In the Three Kingdom Period, a high-type seat *Hu-chuang* (literally bed from non-Han areas), similar to present-day campstool, was introduced for the first time to Han people from the minority nationalities region. As time went by, higher articles for home use such as round stools, square stools started to appear in the Central Plain area. Beds, couches, etc. also became higher gradually,

*Court Music* by Zhou Fang in Tang Dynasty, housed in Taibei Palace Museum.

though low furniture still took a dominant position. Starting from the Western Jin Dynasty, the concept of half-sitting, half-kneeling posture as was required by etiquette, gradually faded. People either sat on the floor with legs stretched out, or sat cross-legged, or sat aslant, just as they pleased. And then the side-table was created which was placed on the bed for leaning against or leaning back, together with *yinnang*, something like a modern back-cushion.

When it came to the Tang Dynasty, people started to sit on a seat instead of sitting on the floor. In the late years of Tang Dynasty, tables and chairs appeared which, though not yet prevalent, had greatly affected people's way of life. Furniture at that time included chiefly side tables, narrow tables, *xieshi* (an article developed from side table used for leaning against), chests, cupboards, *Hu-chuang*, screens, chessboards. High-type furniture such as tables, stools, chairs, etc. already turned up and became popular in the upper circles. By the Song Dynasty, all sorts of high-type furniture started to fall into a pattern and widely used. In the Southern Song Dynasty, furniture was rather complete in variety and shape, the workmanship increasingly exquisite.

By the Ming and Qing dynasties, Chinese ancient furniture became settled into a shape much higher than in the past. The Ming-dynasty furniture looks elegant, plain and ingenious and was commended as brilliant representative of Chinese classic furniture, known as Ming-type furniture. The rise of Ming furniture was closely associated with the social environment of the times, as the booming of cities and towns, the growth of commodity economy and the emergence of architecture in large numbers, made the demand for furniture continuously on the increase. Moreover, in the Ming Dynasty,

Ming-dynasty yellow rosewood mandarin-style chair, 116 cm high, named from its resembling ancient official's headgear.

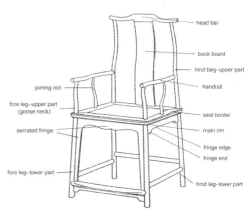

Structural drawing of the mandarin-style chair.

77

Zheng He the great navigator made seven trips to the West and the ban on maritime trade and relations with foreign countries was once lifted, resulting in large quantity of timber brought to China from Southeastern Asia. Besides, woodworking implements had been improved to an extent as never before. The book *Tiangong Kaiwu* (Exploitation of the Works of Nature) records that the forging techniques were already highly promoted in the Ming Dynasty, with it different kinds of woodworking implements were invented, in planes alone there were pushing plane, thin-line plane, centipede plane, etc., to be used for different processes.

*The Canon of Lu Ban* compiled by Wu Rong, head of the imperial workman department under the Board of Works of the Beijing municipal government, is the only extant specialized book about building and repairing of wooden things. The book sums up the designs and practices of master craftsmen over centuries since the Spring and Autumn Period. Included in the book are thirty-plus drafts for furniture in which each measurements, tenon and mortise structure, end of lines and adornments are all given in detail, with real object pictures attached. It is a significant reference material for the study of Ming Dynasty folk architecture and Ming-style furniture.

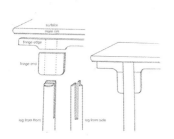

Chuck held: most common tenon-riveting table structure.

In Ming-style furniture making, materials were most particular about. Usually hard wood such as red sandalwood, *huang-hua-li-mu* (a species of rosewood) and the like, was chosen, which when polished with wax, reveals their natural grain and freshening luster , fully in accord with the taste of the men of letters in the Ming Dynasty who are always after primitive simplicity and elegance. As they advocated nature, they preferred yellow color to dark color, and *huang-hua-li-mu* which is fine in grain, having the color of amber and the touch of jade, became the first to be chosen in the late Ming Dynasty down to the early Qing Dynasty.

Furniture making procedures include: to cut open wood, to saw timber, to plane, chisel, drill, carve, polish, lacquer and wax. The precise and ingenious process of fitting a tenon into a mortise to make a joint is a unique feature of Ming-style furniture making in which all joints are formed with tenon and mortise without using nail or glue. Tenon can be

Illustration in *Jin Ping Mei*, a classical Chinese novel.

Ming-dynasty yellow rosewood side table, 113 cm long, 27.7 cm wide, 83 cm high. It is used to place musical instruments in former times.

divided into open tenon, closed tenon, square-and-corner tenon, long-and-short tenon, swallow-tail tenon, etc.

The Qing Dynasty people valued dark color instead of yellow. They were partial to luxury and majesty. As the Qing royal family favored red sandalwood in particular, it became the first choice for the material used in making furniture. The existing articles are mostly from the court, all carved meticulously. In the middle of Qing Dynasty, *huanghuali*, red sandalwood, etc., became extremely in short supply. Then red wood started to be imported and used extensively. Red wood is similar in quality to red sandalwood. It is of hard texture, and appears grand and majestic. Its main disadvantages are such as not tenacious enough to be easily carved and it is susceptible to changing shape when affected with damp, dryness, cold, or heat and is therefore unfit for meticulous carving.

The Ming-style furniture excels in plain shape while the Qing-style one is good at multifarious and elaborate decoration. The crafts in making furniture in the Qing Dynasty were so consummate that they had reached the apex of traditional furniture crafts. Not only had they inherited the traditional methods, but also absorbed exotic culture to form distinctive style of the times.

By the Ming and Qing dynasties, traditional furniture had already completed in varieties, which fell into six major categories: chairs (stool); side tables; cupboards (cabinet); beds (couch); stands (rack) and screens. Chairs include official-headgear shaped chair, rose chair, lamp-hanging chair, round-backed armchair, folding chair, square stool, long stool, drum-shaped stool. Tables include *kang* (a heatable bed commonly used in North China), tea table, incense-burner table, writing desk, flat table, end-upwards table (table with both ends raised upwards), *jiaji* table (table on top of which side table is placed), lute table, altar table, square table, Eight Immortals table (square table seating eight people), crescent table, etc. Cupboards include cupboard-cabinet (combining the functions of cupboard, cabinet and table), *menhu* cupboard (table with drawers, somewhat similar to

Furniture displayed in the back house of Confucian Temple of Qufu, Shandong.

the chest of drawers), wardrobe, bookcase, treasure case, treasure box, etc. Beds include framed bed, wooden couch, etc. Stands include coat hanger, basin stand, lamp-stand, shelf for holding potted flowers, dressing table, foot supporter, etc. And screens include *chaping* (table screen with a stand), *Weiping* (folding screen usu. with four, six or eight folds), *luzuo* (stove base), *huzuo* (pot base), etc. The furniture in the Ming and Qing dynasties often used metals as auxiliary components to further protect and reinforce the furniture, and to add luster as well.

# Gold and Silver Ware, Glassware, Enamelware

## Gold and silver ware

The major methods for processing gold articles originated from bronze making, which include smelting, mould founding, hammering, welding, bead-forming, engraving, wire-drawing, wire-twining, wire inlay, etc., but developed or innovated. Take the bead-forming craft for example. It is an art unique to gold processing in which the first step is to let melted gold drip into warm water drop by drop to form beads of various sizes, and then by welding each tiny drop of gold, fish-egg patterns or bead-string patterns are made. Silverware turned up later than gold, and followed gold articles in working procedures.

From the very beginning gold and silver articles came out as artworks. The existing earliest gold objects were made in the Shang Dynasty more than 3,000 years ago. They were mostly ornaments, simple in shape, small in size, with less decorative patterns. The Shang-dynasty gold articles were chiefly gold and silver foil, gold leaves and sheets, used to adorn utensils; only a few in the northern and northwestern regions were used for personal adornment. Of the earlier gold articles, the gold masks and the gold staffs unearthed from the early Shu-culture ruins in Sanxingdui of Guanghan, Sichuan Province, are the most eye-catching. In the Shang and Zhou dynasties, the bronze techniques and the jade

Eagle decorated golden crown top and golden crown belt of the Warring States Period.

carving both facilitated the growth of gold and silver crafts.

The silver *chuwang yi* (ladle for dipping water in the shape of a gourd used by the king of the State of Chu) kept in the Palace Museum is one of the earliest silver utensils discovered so far. During the Spring and Autumn and Warring States Period, articles with gold and silver inlay came into view in great quantity, which marked the high technical level of gold crafts at that time. The process of gold and silver inlay started from the mid-Spring and Autumn Period, prevailed in the Warring States Period and gradually went downhill since the Western Han Dynasty. It is one of the ancient fine metal techniques used for adornment. The procedure is to incise patterns or inscriptions on the surface of bronzeware by casting or by chiseling, then have gold and silver wire inlaid, and then grind and polish to produce a decorative effect.

In the Han Dynasty, the gold and silver objects, in addition to decorating bronze and iron utensils using such techniques as coating, mounting, plating, inlaying, etc., were applied to lacquer ware and silk fabrics in the shape of foils or filings to increase splendor. Gradually the craft of using gold foil to make flower-shaped patterns grew mature, until it finally broke away from traditional bronze craft to develop all on

Qin-dynasty silver basin, 37 cm in diameter, 5.5 cm high, 1,705g in weight, housed in Shandong Zibo Museum.

its own.

During the Six Dynasties Period, as external exchange expanded and the Buddhist art spread, gold and silver articles used in Buddhism emerged, often giving the alien flavor of the northern nomads or the Persian Sassanids Empire.

The gold and silver articles in the Tang Dynasty were various in kind, including tableware, drinking bowls, vessels, containers for medicine, miscellaneous articles for household use, ornaments and articles for religious use. Moreover, the process in making them was meticulous and complex. Hammering, casting, welding, cutting, polishing, riveting, plating, carving and piercing were extensively used. So resplendent and graceful, so elegant and vivacious, so healthy and mature that had the gold and silver ware already become one of the signs of a prosperous age.

In the Song Dynasty works of gold and silver combined with wood, lacquer and other materials came into being, and the art of painting was introduced for adornment, using solid carving decoration and raised floral-pattern technique. In the Yuan Dynasty, new varieties of artworks were developed including vases, cases, *zun* (a kind of wine vessel in ancient times), *lian* (toilet case used by women), and shelves. In the Ming and Qing dynasties, the gold and silver articles were meticulous in shape and the workmanship was pleasing to the eye. In the Qing Dynasty, the compound process became more developed by which gold, silver combined with enamel, pearl, jade, gem, etc., set one another off to form a bright scene.

Tang-dynasty silver hollow ball-shaped censer-warmer. It is an ingenious device containing a perfume receptacle on an axle which always maintains the same orientation regardless of any movement of the supporting structure.

83

Chinese Arts & Crafts

Yuan-dynasty silver artwork, carved from a dragon-shaped stump. The artifact shows a Taoist priest sitting against a stump reading a book held in hand.

## Glassware

Glass containing lead and barium emerged as early as the Western Zhou Dynasty. The lead-barium glass requires a relatively low melting temperature. It looks sparkling and crystal clear, but thin and brittle, and can not resist sharp drop or rise in temperature. It is therefore unfit for making utensils or apparatuses. Often lead-barium glass was processed to make ornaments, ritual objects or funerary objects.

By the beginning of the Warring States Period, dragonfly-eye and jade-imitation glass was invented. Dragonfly-eye glass is prepared by adhering multicolor rings on top of glass beads, looking like dragonfly-eyes, thus the name. In the Spring and Autumn and Warring States Period, glass techniques became mature and technical exchange with foreign country started. The technical process in making glass includes casting, twining, inlaying, etc. Glass objects such as *bi* (a round piece of jade with a hole in its center used for ceremonial purposes in ancient China), ring and sword are prepared by pouring melted glass into moulds.

In the Han Dynasty, glass manufacturing became poly-centered, mainly in three regions. In the Central Plain region, Zhou Dynasty process was followed, producing chiefly lead-barium glass. In the Hexi Corridor region (in Northwestern Gansu, so called because it lies to the west of the Yellow River)

Dragon-eye glass bead necklace of Warring States Period housed in Hubei Museum. Each bead is 2.5 cm in diameter.

lead-barium glass was also produced with traditional formula, adding sodium and calcium as flux. In the Linnan Region (area covering Guangdong and Guangxi) centered on Guangzhou, potassium-silicon glass was produced. In the Wei, Jin, Northern and Southern dynasties, regional separatist regimes hankered after importing foreign glass, in particular in the Northern Dynasties Period, when the rulers not only imported glass, but also introduced western glass technology to China. In the Sui Dynasty, a eunuch named He Chou, drawing on the experience of green porcelain manufacturing, successfully produced glass. Glass in the Tang Dynasty was mainly high-lead glass without containing barium, but containing sodium sometimes.

Since the Ming and Qing dynasties, glass grew various in kind. In the Ming Dynasty, Yanshen Town (now Yidu of

Sui-dynasty covered pot made of green glass.

Qing-dynasty blue transparent glass bottle kept in Palace Museum.

Shandong Province) was a hub of glass production, where the site of glass furnace ruins that had long fallen into oblivion has now been excavated. The Qing Dynasty was at the zenith of ancient glass manufacturing. Glass production at that time was double centered. In the south was Guangzhou while in the north was Yanshen Town. The imperial glass factory was known for merging together the glass process in the north and south with European techniques. The imperial glass was plain and unsophisticated, unusually exquisite, representing the achievements attained in glass making in the Qing Dynasty.

## Enamelware

The enamelware manufacturing craft is actually a complex process combining enamel process and metal process. It is prepared by first grinding quartz, silicon, feldspar, borax, and some metal minerals into powder and then melting, and then applying on metal utensils to form a surface after baking. Sometimes polishing or gold-plating is needed. Enamelware which has the sturdiness of metal, the smoothness and corrosion-resistance of glass, is practical and beautiful. To date the earliest enamel object made in China is the Tang-dynasty gold-inlaid silver-base enamel mirror now kept in the Shosoin

Repository of Nara, Japan. But no other enamelware was found in the three or four hundred years afterwards. In the late years of the Yuan Dynasty, Chinese enamelware became less influenced by Arabian culture and more and more nationalized.

Enamelware includes gold-inlay enamel, coating enamel, painting enamel in terms of processing methods, and gold-base enamel, copper-base enamel, porcelain-base enamel, glass-base enamel, purple-clay enamel, etc. in terms of bases. Among them the copper-base enamel is the most popular, because the copper price is relatively lower, and enamel is easier to adhere to the copper surface. The distinguished traditional Chinese handicraft Jingtailan (cloisonné enamel), its scientific name being copper background wire-inlay enamel, got its name from being made in large quantities in Beijing during the Jingtai Reign of the Ming Dynasty, and the enamel used was mostly of a blue color. The procedure of Jingtailan includes chiefly base-making, wire-inlaying, firing and soldering, blue enamel coating, enamel-baking, polishing, and gold-plating. Coating is done by using small iron spade or glass tube to apply glaze of different colors first on the background, then on the designs and then finally to apply

Yuan-dynasty pinch-wire elephant-ear heater, housed in Palace Museum. It is a gold gilded copper artwork coated with enamel that looks refined and gorgeous.

Ming-dynasty pinch-wire enamel bottle, housed in Palace Museum.

the blue glaze and add some shiny white substance. Glazing and baking procedure is done repeatedly, one blazing followed by one baking, often three times are needed for quality cloisonné.

Promoted and propped up by the Qing government, the enamel handicraft grew fast in the Qing Dynasty based on the achievements attained during the Yuan and Ming dynasties. In the reign of Emperor Kangxing, an enamel factory was set up in the court, making wire-inlay enamel and base-engraving enamel at first, and then making painted enamel successfully on a tentative basis. Painted enamel which often applies on small objects is heavy and thick in color, similar to the mixed glaze in earlier times. Porcelain-base enamel, also called enameled color porcelain, is to apply enamel paint on porcelain base. It is a perfect combination of porcelain and painted enamel craft. In the reign of Emperor Qianlong, painted enamel craft was booming. Aside from the court, Guangzhou was the major place of painted enamel making. The painted enamel works made in court featured neat design, meticulous painting, and elevated style, using mostly bright yellow color that is rich in royal flavor. Painted

Qing-dynasty enamel landscape heater, housed in Palace Museum.

enamel works made in Guangzhou have bold and unstrained lines, decorated with European-style roll-up leaves design using glaze material imported from western countries that is gorgeous in color and sparkling in luster. At that time, snuff bottles of diversified types meticulously produced showed up. They were produced combining enamel, jade, agate, crystal, and porcelain with calligraphic and drawing art. Even western subject matters such as European women and babies, western styled pavilions and towers, etc. were adopted for designs, which were rarely seen in previous dynasties.

# Bamboo Carving, Wood Carving, Ivory Carving

## Bamboo Carving

Bamboo carving means to carve various ornamental patterns or characters on bamboo items, or make ornaments from bamboo roots by carving. China is the first country in the world using bamboo articles. The extant bamboo carving item early in age is the painted lacquer bamboo ladle unearthed from the Western Han Tombs No.1 in Mawangdui of Changsha. Decorated with dragon and braids designs using bas-relief and fretwork techniques, it is a highly finished rarity.

Since the mid-Ming Dynasty, bamboo carving developed into a special art. At the very beginning, there were only a few well-educated artisans working for bamboo carving. As bamboo was easily available, more and more people started to join in this craft, some by handing down from father to son, some by passing on from master to apprentice, some by learning from others privately, until bamboo carving became a special line with a great quantity of works left over to posterity. Bamboo joint carving is the representative variety in bamboo carving in which bamboo joints are shaped into brush pots, incense tubes, tea caddies, etc. and then its surface pierced out to make relief sculpture to produce an artistic

Ming-dynasty brush pot, housed in Nanjing Museum.

effect.

The techniques of bamboo carving mainly include keeping green-covering, pasting yellow chips, round carving and inlaying.

The craft of keeping green covering refers to that motifs are carved using bamboo surface layer hull with other part on the surface removed. That part, appearing pale yellow, is called bamboo muscle, which is used as background. When a bamboo is dried, its outer layer gradually turns from green to light yellow, and then remains unchanged. But the bamboo muscle will change from light yellow first to deep yellow, then to reddish purple with color and luster growing deeper and deeper until they resemble amber's. When the bamboo muscle is often stroked with hand, it will become smooth and mild. As time goes by, the outer layer and the bamboo muscle differ distinctly in luster and color, and the designs become more and more clear.

Qing-dynasty brush pot with a relief showing a monk carrying a staff, housed in Palace Museum.

The yellow chip (bamboo muscle) refers to the light yellow inner layer of the bamboo. It is glossy and smooth, like ivory. In the craft of pasting yellow chips, large bamboos from the south are used as material. Fresh yellow chips are boiled, dried in the air, flattened by pressing, and then paste onto the surface of objects made of various materials. Often wooden articles are used, among which Chinese littleleaf box which is fine in texture and similar to bamboo yellow chips in color and luster, is the best choice. Sometimes two or three layers of yellow chips are pasted as required by design so as to make several patterns closely linked up as if wrought through the invisible hand of nature. The technique of pasting yellow chips prevailed in the Qing Dynasty in many places across the country.

In round carving craft bamboo roots are often used. The design is based on the natural shape of the roots on which carving or piercing is applied slightly to make ingenious ornaments that appear unsophisticated. At that time, the Feng family in Jiading was the most distinguished of round carving who inherited the techniques from Zhu family. The works they made, using bamboo roots as material, imitating nature in design, were known for being original in shape and glowing with radiance and vitality.

In order to add a sense of gradation in wood and bamboo carving, the inlay process is used in which designs are formed with materials of different textures and colors, or a "treasure inlaid artwork" is created with jade, stone, bamboo, wood, bone, etc. set onto a single piece of work.

## Wood Carving

Woodcarving in China constitutes three major categories: architecture carving, furniture carving and artworks carving. Woodcarving as handiworks for display or fondling started from the Song Dynasty when the practice of fondling artworks gradually rose among men of letters and refined scholars. This prevailing custom reached its climax in the Ming and Qing dynasties. Furnishing artworks are a traditional category in wood carving, which are placed on cabinets, windowsills, tables, shelves, etc. Wood carving can also be used to decorate all sorts of furniture and other artworks such as jade-ware, cloisonné and chinaware.

Woodcarving can be seen all over the region on both sides of the Yangtze River where the best known includes the Dongyang woodcarving in Zhejiang Province, the golden-lacquer woodcarving in Guangdong Province, longan woodcarving in Fujian Province and Huizhou woodcarving in Anhui Province.

Dongyang County of Zhejiang Province has always been celebrated for being the "home of carving." Dongyang woodcarving started from the Tang Dynasty, developed in the Song Dynasty and became popular in the Ming and Qing dynasties. Dongyang carvings preserve the original textures

Qing-dynasty carved bamboo loop-handle pot, housed in Palace Museum.

91

Ming-dynasty eaglewood
mandarin duck hand warmer,
5 cm high, 6.5 cm long, 6.5 cm
wide.

and colors of the wood which, when meticulously polished, make the finished works appear smooth and lustrous. Relief carving is the essence of Dongyang woodcarving in which the depth of the patterns ranges between two and five millimeters. The centerpiece is focused on by the force of the cutting. The designs of Dongyang woodcarving lays stress on "carving all over the background," which means to have patterns carved over the entire surface of the object so that it has three dimensional display while the background is fully covered. That is a unique artistic style.

Gold lacquer woodcarving is a specialty of the Chaozhou region in Guangdong Province, otherwise known as Chaozhou woodcarving, so named because of the gold coating on the surface. Gold lacquer woodcarving at first was a decorative art used in architecture in ancient China. Later on it was influenced by local art and became a school of woodcarving featuring local flavor. In Chaozhou, local people have specially compounded a kind of lacquer which not only enables the gold foil to adhere to the surface of the wood, but also makes it moisture-proof and rot-proof. The history of Chaozhou woodcarving can be traced back to the Tang Dynasty and earlier. The Qing Dynasty is the heyday of its development when the fretwork developed from single-layer to multi-layer piercing, producing thus an artistic effect of a strong contrast between far and near, large and small.

Fujian longan (Euphoria longan, evergreen tree) carving developed from furniture decoration and statue-of-Buddha

*Cow Suckling its Calf,* Chinese littleleaf box wood carving, 8 cm high, 12.3 cm long, housed in Palace Museum.

carving, matured around the end of Ming Dynasty and the beginning of Qing Dynasty. Longan is slightly brittle in texture, fine grained, reddish brown in color, mainly growing in the southern area of Fujian Province. The trunk in particular the roots of old-age longan, often grows to be either spectacular or grotesque, which is an ideal wood for engraving. Root carving therefore becomes the unique variety of Fuzhou woodcarving. Local artisans, making the best use of its natural shape, by chopping with axe or cutting with chisel, have the twisted roots with their rough nodes carved into all sorts of figures, birds and beasts in shapes vivid and artistically exaggerated. Fuzhou woodcarving when smoothed and polished can reveal unsophisticated brass yellow or orange color that will never fade.

Wood used in Huizhou woodcarving includes soft or less hard species such as pine, China fir, camphor tree, nanmu, gingko, etc. What Huizhou woodcarving stresses is not the quality of wood, but the content of subject matters, the skills at carving, and the perfection of composition and lines, which has exerted a great influence on the surrounding areas. In the Ming and Qing dynasties, Huizhou woodcarving is focused on architecture and furniture decoration, well-known for its giant-sized carved paintings whose themes are mostly "men farming and women weaving," fishing, woodcutting, plowing, studying, fairy tales, legends, historical stories, classic novels, and so on and so forth.

## Ivory Carving

Early in the Neolithic Age, the Chinese ancients already started to use articles made of bones, fangs, and horns from animals along with stoneware, wooden articles and pottery ware. Materials for carving taken from animals are mostly ivory. The animal-mask patterned ivory cup inlaid with pine-and-stone design unearthed from the Fuhao Tomb

Shang-dynasty ivory carving: *kuipan* (dragon-like monopode animal) cup unearthed from the Fuhao tomb at Yin Ruins, Anyang, Henan, housed in the National Museum of China.

94

in the Yin Ruins, Henan in 1976 can be called a representative of the Shang Dynasty ivory carving.

The ivory carving craft made rapid progress in the Song Dynasty, marked by the multi-cased ivory ball named "Superlative Workmanship" using fretwork process completed by the royal handicraft workshop. On the surface of the ball relief patterns are engraved; inside the ball are several hollow balls with different size one on top of the other. Each ball is engraved with exquisite and complicated designs, appearing delicate and refined.

In the Ming and Qing dynasties, economic and cultural exchanges with South Asia and Africa promoted. Ivory material was introduced to China. Then the ivory carving art entered a period of full bloom.

In the Ming Dynasty, ivory carving was mainly done in Beijing, Yangzhou and Guangzhou, and widely involved by the government, folk artisans, men of letters and refined scholars. Ivory artworks and other small-sized carved articles using bamboo, wood, gold, stone, etc. became rare curios and ornaments. At that time ivory and rhinoceros horn carvings made no difference to bamboo, wood, gold or stone carving so far as carving skills were concerned. Quite a number of craftsmen had no difficulty in carving using different materials, some were known as all-arounders in carving.

In addition to the common techniques such as single-line intaglio carving, round carving, relief carving, micro-carving, etc., there are three more unique skills in Chinese ivory carving: fretwork, cleaving-plaiting and inlaying-dyeing.

The most typical of fretwork item is the intricate hollowed out ivory balls. Some have dozens layers, cased one on top of another, each able to revolve. It is the quintessence of Chinese culture. The working procedures of cleaving-plaiting is, by making use of ivory's properties of marvelous tenacity and fine grain, cleave ivory into even thin pieces and then plait into artworks such as mattresses, round fans, flower baskets, lampshades, etc. As ivory can only be cleaved into fine pieces in an environment with a temperate and moist climate, this kind of craft naturally becomes exclusive to the southern regions. Inlaying-dyeing craft has two different

Ming-dynasty ivory carving: human figure, 20 cm high, housed in Shanghai Museum.

Qing-dynasty ivory filament plaited round fan housed in Palace Museum. It features the cleave-plaiting craft unique to Guangdong ivory carving.

Ivory carving of twelve
Chinese zodiac signs.

forms. One is to inlay other gorgeously colored substance on the surface of ivory items; the other is to inlay ivory pieces together with other bright substance such as precious stone, on designed patterns. Dyeing is able to improve the monotonous color, and to cover the defects of ivory, horn, etc. Inlay-dyeing enhanced the decorative effect of ivory carving items, making them more brilliant and graceful, more splendorous and colorful.

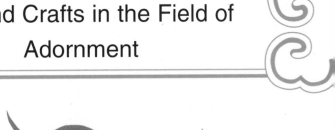

# Arts and Crafts in the Field of Adornment

# Jade Artwork

Jade has been cherished by the Chinese as a symbol of many virtues. Its hardness suggests firmness and loyalty, and its luster projects purity and beauty. Typical subjects are carvings of flowers, animals, vases, and human figures.

In the Neolithic Age, when people gradually recognized colored stone similar to jade in choosing stone for making implements, they used such stone to make implements, ornaments and sacrificial offerings. The colored stone turned items can be called the embryonic form of jade artworks, which can be traced back to the Hemudu Culture in China. By the middle and late years of the Neolithic Age, jade-carving had been detached from stone ware making to become an independent handicraft. China is a major jade producer in the world. According to *Shan Hai Jing* (Book on Mountains and Seas), an ancient writing about geography, there are more than two hundred places where jade is found, which means that the source of jade is inexhaustible in China. Hetian of Xinjiang is a well-known place of jade origin in China; Jiuquan of Gansu, Lantian of Shaanxi, Dushan and Mixian of Henan, and Xiuyan of Liaoning are also rich in quality jade resources.

Generally, the procedure of jade carving includes jade

Jade pendant of the Hemudu Culture, one of the earliest discovered so far.

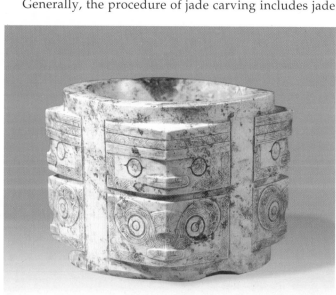

Animal-mask patterned *cong* (long hollow piece of jade) of the Liangzhu Culture, 8.8 cm high, about 6,500g in weight.

Western Han-dynasty jade cladding, a funerary object carved out of a whole piece of jade into a dozen or so pieces for each correspondent part of the face.

observation, designing, opening, piercing, cutting and polishing. Tang Rongzuo, a collector in the late Qing Dynasty, once wrote a book entitled *Of Jade* in which the working procedure, methods and implements in carving jade ware are illustrated with twelve color drawings. As viewed from the perspective of craft, a jade artwork with superb workmanship excelling nature is not made by carving, but by grinding with water using minerals such as emery, silicon, garnet, etc. that are harder than jade. Therefore the process of jade making is called jade rolling or jade grinding. While the skills in grinding jade are superb, the tools used are simple and crude. The primitive implement used is simply a revolving round disk called *tuo* (emery wheel), which is used to move emery which rubs, smoothes and polishes jade. During the Neolithic Age and the Bronze Age when ironware was not yet been invented, tools used were largely made from wood, bamboo, animal bone compounded with sandstone. Until the modern times, Chinese people always used

Jade Carving: an illustration in *Tiangong Kaiwu* (Exploitation of the Works of Nature).

99

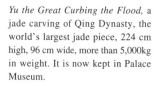

*Yu the Great Curbing the Flood,* a jade carving of Qing Dynasty, the world's largest jade piece, 224 cm high, 96 cm wide, more than 5,000kg in weight. It is now kept in Palace Museum.

traditional tools in the manufacture of jade artworks such as wire saw, round disc made of steel and wrought iron, etc.

Jade carving was highly developed in the Han and Tang dynasties. Funerary jade was the most typical of the Han jade articles. It was made in the belief that the jade would keep the body from decaying. Funerary jade articles include jade apparel, nine orifice stopper, etc. The jade apparel was divided into gold inlaid, silver inlaid and copper inlaid prepared in the light of the identity and official title of the dead. The nine orifice stopper was used to cover the nine orifices of the ears, eyes, mouth, nostrils, anus and genital in the hope that the body would not decay as the vital energy was preserved by the orifice stoppers. As regards jade articles for ornament, jade galloping steeds, jade bears, jade eagles, and jade *bi xie* (a legendary holy beast, looking like a lion, with two wings, said

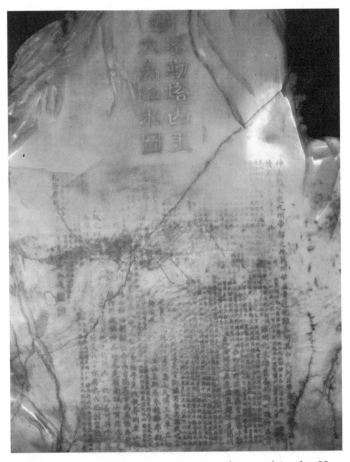

Inscriptions on the back of *Yu the Great Curbing the Flood.*

to drive out evil things), were manufactured in the Han Dynasty. These artworks were practical in shape, exquisite in workmanship, and unconstrained in style. The Tang Dynasty jade artworks, affected by painting, sculpture, and the art of the Western Region, were represented by the eight-petal pattern jade cup and animal mask agate cup, in a style dignified and stately, full of Western Region flavor.

Circumstances change with the passage of time, from the Song-Liao-Jin Period the function of jade objects as sacrificial vessels was weakened, and instead, jade artworks close to practical life, some for ornaments and some for daily appreciation dominated with the prosperity of urban economy. In the Song Dynasty, the "qiao se"(wise use of color) process was initiated by which various objects extremely refined could be carved in the light of the natural

*Du Shan Yu Hai* (Extra large jade of Dushan), a jade carving of Yuan Dynasty, 70 cm high, 493 cm in circumference.

*Du Shan Yu Hai* (partial).

luster and color of the jade material, and its texture and shape.

The Yuan, Ming and Qing dynasties were the heyday of jade carving. Du Shan Yu Hai (extra large jade bowl of Dushan) and Da Yu Zhi Shui Yu Shan (Jade Mountain: Yu the Great Curbing Flood) were two representative pieces of the time. The artwork Du Shan Yu Hai was carved following the natural shape of the jade material to form a scene where auspicious animals swimming at will over the waves, reflecting considerably the heroic spirit of the Yuan people. The work Da Yu Zhi Shui Yu Shan manifests the influence of literati painting on artworks taking the Song Dynasty painting Yu the Great Curbing the Flood as master copy.

# Paper-cut

Paper cutting is a long-standing decorative folk art in China. The cutter first draws the designs on a piece of paper and then cuts it out with scissors or a knife. In the countryside, paper cuts are often stuck on windows and doors as auspicious and joyful decorations to mark festivals and happy occasions. Often decorative patterns like baby, gourd, lotus, etc. can be used to symbolize plenty of offspring and plenty of blessings. As a type of folk art, paper cutting evinces distinctive local features: unpretentious and uninhibited as in Shaanxi; graceful and fine as in Hebei; resplendent and orderly as in Sichuan; exquisite and pleasing as in Jiangsu. Paper cuts are also used for decorating gifts or as a gift itself.

Blocking flower papercut of Northern Dynasty, stored in Xinjiang Uygur Autonomous Region Museum: It is the earliest papercut discovered so far.

There are two chief crafts in preparing paper cutting, the scissor-cutting approach and the knife-cutting approach. Just as the terms suggest, with the scissor-cutting approach, the scissors are sued as tool. Component parts of a pattern are cut at first and paste into a whole, and then clip the pattern with sharp scissors to make a fine finish. By knife-cutting approach a paper is folded into several layers, which is placed on a soft mixture of ash and animal fat, and then cut carefully with a small knife. In comparison with scissor cutting, knife cutting can have more patterns cut at one time.

With reference to the skills, paper cutting falls into cut-in-relief, intaglio and mixed carving. The relief cutting process is a development of traditional Chinese linear pattern tracing approach. Works done using such approach are extraordinary exquisite with the lines cut as fine as hair. By intaglio the images appear more dignified and unaffected with bright spots or white lines incised into dark surface. The mixed carving using relief cutting and incised cutting alternatively, further enriched paper-cut manifestation. With respect to coloring, there are multicolor cutting, dyeing cutting and golden color cutting. By multicolor cutting, more than two polychrome sheets are put together to form a pattern before cutting. By dyeing cutting, dyeing liquid is dripped onto

*Eight Immortals Celebrating Birthday*, a Beijing painted papercut of Qing Dynasty, collected by Wang Shucun.

*Eight Immortals*, a figure papercut of Huangxian, Shandong in Qing Dynasty, kept in Shandong Art Gallery.

finished paper-cuts. The permeability of water can make the different colors seeping into each other without being confused, thus producing a bright and gorgeous effect. By golden color cutting, patterns are cut using golden paper and then set off with all sorts of colored paper so as to appear resplendent and magnificent, suitable for festival decoration.

The art of paper cutting in China came into being during the Han and Wei period before iron tools and paper were invented. Much earlier before that, carving craft had made rapid growth. The unearthed gold and silver thin sheets used as ornaments in the Warring States Period are similar to paper in shape. In the Western Han Dynasty, people started to make paper using hemp fibers. Legend has it that Emperor Wu of Han Dynasty (156-87 B.C.) who missed incessantly his favorite concubine Lady Li, gave an order to a sorcerer to carve a figure of Lady Li with hemp paper in order to call back the spirits of the dead lady. That is perhaps the earliest paper-cut. The two round pieces of flower-patterned paper-cut of the Northern and Southern Dynasties unearthed from the old city of Gaochang, Xinjiang, are the earliest paper-cut works in China up to now. They were cut from hemp paper, in folded shape, used as sacrificial offerings, showing excellent craftsmanship of the artists.

Paper making was highly developed in the Song Dynasty. Paper of every description was created one after another, contributive greatly to the enrichment of paper-cut varieties, such as paper cuts for window decoration, for lantern ornament, for teacup adornment, etc. From the Song Dynasty paper cutting had also become an applied art. For instance, paper-cut designs were used for ceramics in the Jizhou kilns in Jiangxi Province. The process is to paste paper-cut works on china wares in the course of glazing before baking in the kiln. This kind of craft has the advantage of having designs vivid and lively. The application of paper-cut further expanded in the Song Dynasty. It was used to cut shadow play figures out of hides of animals such as donkey, ox, horse and sheep. By that time, professional craftsmen specialized in paper-cutting appeared, each having his own strong point, some good at cutting calligraphic works of all schools; some well versed in cutting all sorts of designs. In the book entitled *Zhiyatang Zachao* (Miscellaneous Records of Lofty Aspiration Hall) written by Zhou Mi (1232-c. 1298) of the Song Dynasty, a man named Yu Jingzhi was mentioned, and he was the first artisan recorded in the history of paper-cut.

In the Ming and Qing dynasties the art of paper-cut reached a period of full bloom. It was applied on the folk lanterns, covering of fans, embroidered fabrics, etc. For example, the running horse lantern in the Ming Dynasty is a kind of decorative lantern with a revolving circle of colorful paper-cut horses and other figures, which revolves as hot air ascends from the candle burning within it. Paper-cut works are more commonly used for household decoration, beautification of living environment, etc.

Paper-cut artisans are mainly women. Being good at needlework is traditionally an important sign of female perfection. Paper-cut is also included in the category of needlework and is a must for girls to learn since childhood. Through imitative cutting, repeated cutting, drawing-and-

*Aihu* (cloth tiger filled with moxa), a folk papercut of Shandong Penglai, used to paste on the door on Dragon Boat Festival.

*Mouse Stealing Oil*, a Shaanxi papercut used for window decoration.

Papercut: Chinese zodiac signs.

cutting, starting from familiar objects such as fish, insects, birds, animals, flowers, plants, pavilions, bridges, scenery, etc., they gradually succeed in mastering this kind of art till they are able to cut new designs spontaneously following their own inclinations.

# New Year Picture

New Year picture is an image carrier of the Spring Festival culture. In China, by the close of the year, New Year pictures are pasted in many places to add auspicious atmosphere. As an age-old art, New Year pictures give expressions to the lifestyle and features of the people, their sentiments and aesthetic tastes. New Year pictures fall into three types in terms of working process: prints, carved paper and paper drawn. Prints mainly refer to ancient woodcut print. The working process includes primarily drawing draft, sketching outline, woodcutting, making plates, printing, painting and framing. Carved paper refers to carving patterns on paper, which gives a fine and vivid picture. Paper drawn, or gray put, refers to a special craft in which the artists use charcoal sticks to draw draft of lines, and then put drawing paper on the draft, by applying willow branch burning ash on it and copy, a few copies can be produced from each draft. To produce a beautiful painting, a set of processes have to be followed including coloring, lining in black, opening the facial features, rinsing hand, etc. "Gray put" pictures began to surface during the Chenghua Period (1465-1487) and became influential later on. The Japanese ukiyoe had assimilated the essence of the techniques of gray put.

*Spending Winter Days*: New Year Painting of Wuqiang, Hebei in Qing Dynasty.

The New Year Pictures originated from the door-god just like the spring couplets. According to the book *Du Duan* by Cai Yi (132-192) of the Eastern Han Dynasty, the pictures of Shen Tu and Yu Lei, two gods guarding the gateway to the high spirits were pasted on the doors of the ordinary people. It was said that when Emperor Taizong of Tang Dynasty fell ill, he heard ghosts and monsters wail outside his sleeping quarters which disturbed his sleep all through the night.

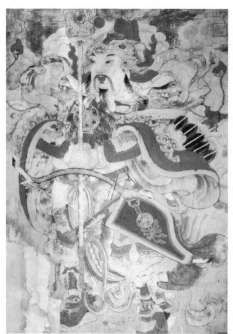

New Year picture of Ming Dynasty: *Door Gods Qin Shubao and Wei Chigong*, painted with meticulous brushwork in rich colors, specially prepared for the aristocrats at that time.

Knowing this, the two senior generals, Qin Shubao and Wei Chigong, offered to stand guard at the royal palace, one holding a sword, and the other two iron staffs. Later on, the emperor had the pictures of these two generals drawn and pasted them on the palate gate. Since then, the custom of pasting door gods spread among the people. One is Qin Shubao, white faced with phoenix eyes, holding two maces; the other is Wei Chigong, black faced with round eyes, holding double iron-staffs.

When printing block carving craft was created in the Song Dynasty, woodcut print made much improvement. New Year pictures henceforth started to develop ever increasingly in both functions and contents. At first, the subject matters were mostly talismans to obviate evil spirits, and then auspiciousness, longevity, blessings, etc. were added to express fine wishes for the coming year. At the same time, folk tales, stories were included, depicting real life of ordinary farmers. The earliest extant New Year picture is the "Picture of Four Peerless Beauties" of the Southern Song Dynasty, the four beauties referring to Wang Zhaojun, Ban Ji, Lü Zhu and Zhao Feiyan, who are known to every household.

In the dynasties of Ming and Qing, artists were keen on New Year picture drawing. The themes used cover jubilation, evil exorcising, customs, scenery, flower-and-bird, court ladies on spring outing, etc. In the last years of Ming Dynasty, New Year pictures has become a genre of painting. Since the prosperous period of Qianlong and Jiaqing, three major centers of New Year pictures gradually came into being: Tianjin Yangliuqing, Shandong Weifang, Yangjiabu and Jiangsu Suzhou Taohuawu.

Yangliuqing New Year pictures started from the last years of Ming Dynasty and prospered from the Yongzheng (1723-1735) to the Guangxu (1875-1908) reign. Yangliuqing New Year pictures depict a wide variety of themes of which the most typical includes "Busy Farming," "Lantern Festival Celebration," "Autumn River Night Crossing," "Visiting Old Acquaintance," "New Year More Auspicious, Family Reunion Fully Comfortable," etc.. The front-end process of Yangliuqing pictures is similar to other woodcut pictures, including writing draft, dividing plates, carving plates, process printing, painting, framing, etc. The later stage work manifests distinctive local features in that stresses are laid on hand painting, and that the carving skills are ingeniously merged with brushwork in painting, making the two arts complement each other.

Yangjiabu woodcut New Year pictures, starting from the last years of Ming Dynasty and flourishing in Qing Dynasy, has a history of over four hundred years. It was in the prime in the Qianlong reign. At that time, the Yangjiabu Village was

*Ten Thousand Tael of Gold*: auspicious painting of Suzhou, Jiangsu, in Qing Dynasty.

化鱣龍魚

*Fish Changed into Dragon*, a New Year picture of Yangliuqing, Tianjin, in Qing Dynasty.

*109*

*Men Busy on Ten Fete Days; Women Busy on Ten Fete Days*: folk blockwood New Year paintings of Shandong Weifang in Qing Dynasty.

known as having "hundred picture shops, thousand picture types and ten thousand printing plates," with dozens of million pictures sold annually, well matched with Tianjin Yangliuqing and Suzhou Taohuawu. Yangjiabu pictures feature lively story, exquisite ornament and lasting appeal, suited to public taste and convenient in printing as well.

Taohuawu woodcut New Year pictures are chief folk woodcut pictures in the region south of the Yangtze, so named because the pictures are produced in a place called Taohuawu in the northern outskirts of Suzhou. In the Hongzhi Period (1488-1505) of Ming Dynasty, the artist Tang Yin (1470-1523) built a cottage named Taohua Hut, hence the name Taohuawu. Taohuawu New Year pictures originated from the carving printing craft in the Song Dynasty, derived from embroidered portraits. It developed into a genre of folk arts in the Ming Dynasty and flourished in the reign of Yongzheng and Qianlong. The pictures feature symmetric composition, resplendent coloring, diversified themes including tales, dramas, social etiquettes, current affairs, news, beauties, babies, even kitchen god, holy horses, etc..

# Arts and Crafts in the Field of
# Entertainment

# Toy

Since ancient times to this day, toys have always accompanied human life. Early in the Neolithic Age, primitive toys already emerged. Folk toys in China have existed for a long time, spread to a wide area, with diversified types and styles made from numerous raw materials. In terms of functions they fall into seasonal toys, intelligence improving toys, acoustic toys, keeping-fit toys, toys for viewing and enjoying, and practical toys. In terms of materials used, they can be divided into clay toys, cloth toys, bamboo and wooden toys, paper toys, etc.

Seasonal toys are closely connected with folkways, subject to a certain season or festival time. Firecrackers and fireworks are special for Spring Festival; running horse lantern and auspicious image lanterns for Lantern Festival; lotus lantern for Spirit Festival; sachet, cloth tiger, moxa-filled figure, five-filament whistle for Dragon-boat Festival; grandpa rabbit for Mid-Autumn Festival; kite for Pure Brightness; etc. Educational toys can arouse people's curiosity and encourage creativity such as tangram, informative map, playing card, small game "puzzle," nine-circle puzzle, Lubanga lock, problem palace rearrangement. Acoustic toys such as earthen whistle, china whistle, diabolo, wheels (wooden shaft at either end of a disk), rattle-drum, tiny gong and drum, glass trumpet, etc., can send out sounds, suitable for babies. Toys for viewing and enjoying are mainly for

Han-dynasty red pottery acrobat figurines.

Painted cloth tigers in
Qing Dynasty.

decoration, such as wood carvings, stone carvings, front-stone carvings, clay figures, wax figures, dough figurines, etc. Keeping-fit toys are mostly for outdoor activities such as Cuju (ancient game similar football), rope skipping, shuttlecock, swing, pot vote (a throwing game). Practical toys can also be used as dress, bedding, food, such as tiger-head shoes, tiger-head cap, sugar figuring, flower face (a kind of bun), etc.. Details are given to some of the above-mentioned toys as below.

Clay toys are the kind the oldest, most wide spread, most highly yielded, and most closely related to folkways. It can be traced back to the Neolithic Age some five or six thousand years ago. By the Eastern Han dynasty, clay toys and earthen toys had already become popular. The earliest toys still in existence are the Tang Dynasty clay figurines. In 1973, large quantity of rare cultural relics of the Tang Dynasty were unearthed from the ancient tombs in Astana, Xinjiang in which a group of four painted laboring clay figurines from Tomb No. 201, vivid and natural in shaping, give a truthful representation of the scene of food preparation at that time. From the Song Dynasty, clay toys turned into commodity with professional artisans specialized in toy making appeared and itinerant peddlers and street stalls could be commonly seen. Clay toys were spread to almost every region where they became closely connected with local conditions and customs.

Wuxi Huishan clay figurines originated in the Ming

Dynasty is the representative of clay toys in China. The clay is taken from the foot of Huishan Hill which is of a unique delicate texture. It is said the area where Huishan clay is obtained covers merely a little over one hectare of land. The figurine production procedure combines molding with painting including soil filtering, soil hammering, drafting, molding, shaping, smoothing, painting, facial making up, oiling, etc. In most cases clay toys are made by mold. First molds are made according the original shape, and then clay bodies are impressed with mold. The bodies are hollow so as to reduce weight and save material. The basic color is often white, with "halo retreat" technique used to make color vary from deep to shallow.

At the early stage Huishan clay figurines centered on toys for kids, produced with molds, simply painted, represented by Da Afu. A folk tale widely circulated about Afu says that many years ago there in the Huishan region ran amuck a wild beast, endangering children. A child named Sha who fought courageously with the fierce beast and eliminated the evil creature. In memory of him people molded a figure of him using the clay taken from Huishan. Many years have passed. Though the images of Afu differ in the hands of different craftspeople through the ages, the basic shape remains a plump full-grown doll in a jacket bearing five characters *fu* (blessing), with a lion in hug, looked serene, smile disclosed, honest, sincere and dignified. The message Da Afu brings is always *fu*, meaning blessing.

Rattle-drum is a representative of acoustic toys in the shape of a drum having a handle, with two small balls attach at either side by a string, which strike the drum when the handle is turned to and fro. The drum is made from wood or bamboo, covered with sheep hide, ox hide or snake skin, etc. among which the one with wooden frame and sheep hide membrane is the most typical. Rattle-drum is the earliest ancient Chinese toy, appeared in the Warring States Period.

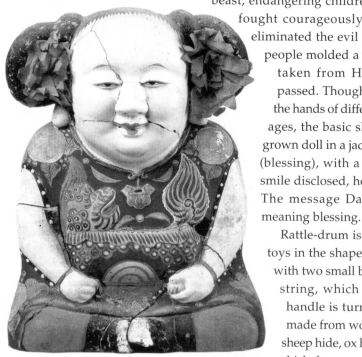

Qing-dynasty Wuxi clay figurines *Da Afu*: an exquisitely painted hollow thin-bodied work.

Toy stall.

It was first used for ceremonial purpose, and later on became an acoustic apparatus when it went to the ordinary people. As it can send out light and merry sound to attract people's attention, it was used by vendors to solicit customers. It is also an ideal toy for infants, helping to temper their grasping and holding strength as well as to test their hearing and sense of touching. Through two thousand years, the shape of rattle-drum as a combination of toy and musical instrument has seldom changed. The rattle-drum as seen in the pictures in the past dynasties is nearly the same as it is today.

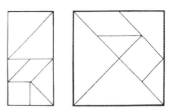

Tangram: an educational toy.

Educational toy in China can be classified into board-type, chess-type, ring-type, card-type and block-moving-type among which, the board-type toys were mostly created by ancient scholars, improved constantly to become mature and welcomed by great masses of people. Board-type toys include primarily Tangram, informative map, 16-*qiao* plate, 21-*qiao* plate, etc. Tangram is a most important jigsaw puzzle consisting of seven thin plates placed in a square or rectangle, which when separated and fixed together again, different patterns can be formed. Tangram was derived from the Song

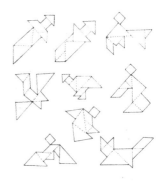

Patterns formed by reassembling the tangram.

*115*

Dynasty "swallow pattern" invented by Huang Bosi who used six rectangular tables and a small side-table to form a swallow-shaped pattern. The pattern gradually spread across the north and south of China, even to the West where it was praised as Tangram, meaning Chinese pattern.

## Kite

Kite is one of the most typical Chinese folk toys. It incorporates into a whole appreciation, entertainment, competition, exercise, and is closely connected with folkways, festivals, science and technology, history, etc., fully revealing the rich content of folk toys. Flying kites often occurs on the occasion when people go for an outing around the Pure Brightness Day. In the past people used to write their own names on the kite when they were in distress or fell ill. As the kite was flying high above, they cut the string and let the kite fly away with the wind. In so doing they believed that their bad luck had gone with the kite.

The name of kite varied in different period of times. Some ancient book written in the pre-Qin period records that the

Flower-basket kite made from *juan*-silk and bamboo in Weifang, Shandong.

New Year's painting: *Kids Flying Kite.*

thinker Mo-tzu and the master craftsman Gongshu Ban had both made something called "wooden hawk." Later on it was said that the distinguished general Han Xin (?-196 B.C.) ever made "paper hawks" in the first years of Han Dynasty. According to more reliable source, the kite originated in the Northern and Southern Dynasties. It was named "paper crow" or "paper owl" at that time. The kite was not used as a toy but used in military affairs, correspondence, measurement, publicity, etc. It was after the Five Dynasties that the kite became popular and turned to be a means of entertainment. During the mid-Tang Dynasty, paper started to be more widely used in everyday life and gradually replaced other more expensive materials in making kite thanks to its low cost and easy working process.

By the Song Dynasty, kite-flying was popularized; kite-making became an occupation. Gradually the custom of flying kites at the Pure Brightness Festival was established. Scenes of flying-kite can be seen in both the famous painting *Pure Brightness Day on the River* by Zhang Zeduan, eminent artist of the Northern Song Dynasty and the picture *One Hundred Sub-graphs* by Su Hanchen.

Kite-flying had its heyday in the dynasties of Ming and Qing. Kids competing in flying kites became a spring-time scene. Even high officials and noble lords enjoyed flying kites. In the Palace Museum in Beijing there are still three big kites

*Enjoying Paper-Hawk Flying*, an illustration in the late-Qing picture album *Painting Treasure of Wu Youru*.

housed that had been played by Puyi, last emperor of Qing Dynasty. Cao Xueqin (1715-1763), the literary giant who wrote the masterpiece *The Dream of Red Mansions*, also wrote a book entitled *Records of Crafts in Making Kites in the North and South*, which contains primarily rhymes about making kites and colored patterns of all types of kites.

Making a kite usually has four steps: making framework, pasting paper, painting and flying. The materials used are usually bamboo, paper, silk fabrics, etc. The shape of the kite was exquisite at first, but later on more realistic style has been developed. The structure of the kite is required to conform not only to the principle of balance, but the principle of aerodynamics so that the kite can fly high above and accomplish all sorts of elegant movements. For instance, the centipede-shaped kite is required to hold its head high; the double-butterfly roll up and down, to the left and to the right; eagle soar and circle, big-board hawk firm as Mount Tai in the sky. The New Year picture workshops at that time used woodblock to print color paper specifically for kite use, whereas artisans decorated kites with various techniques such as pasting paper, making relief from paper, paper-cut, outlining design in gold, etc.

Kite as an entertainment device appealing to both the refined and the ordinary people, has developed a wide range

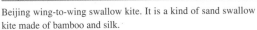

Beijing wing-to-wing swallow kite. It is a kind of sand swallow kite made of bamboo and silk.

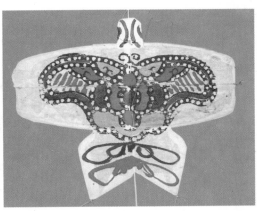

Butterfly kite made of paper and bamboo in Chengdu, Sichuan.

of variety including toy kites, ornamental kites, stunt kites, practical kites in terms of function; hard-wing kites, soft-wing kites, bat-shaped kites, straight-stringed kites, barrel-shaped kites, kites carrying pole, soft kites, etc. in terms of structure; bird-shaped kites, insect-shaped kites, aquatic-shaped kites, human figure kites, character-shaped kites, object-shaped kites, geometric figure kites, etc. in terms of shapes and themes. In the northern and southern regions of the Yangtze River there are kite making centers of which the most distinguished are Beijing, Tianjin, Shandong Weifang, Jiangsu Yangzhou, and Sichuan Chengdu.

Hard-wing kite is a common type of which the two wings are made of bamboo strips connected to the trunk and are non-foldable. Beijing sand-swallow kite is the most typical of hard-wing kites. Its wings are bound with two bamboo strips, one above and the other underneath. The head and the abdomen are formed by bending a long bamboo strip into a U-shape; the tail is made of two bamboo strips crossing each other. Together these parts are bound to form a framework of which each part has fixed proportion in measurement. Hard-wing kite is easy to make, solid and durable, and is therefore favored by many people.

Bat-shaped kite looks like a flat board in the shape of a mask, a tripod, or a cicada, etc. The most characteristic is the traditional Eight Trigrams kite, which has to rely on strong wind force to fly up in the sky. The bat-shaped kites can be

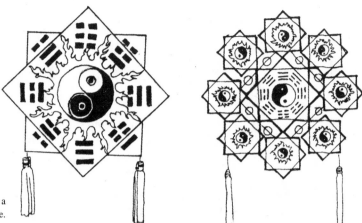

Eight Trigrams kite: a
type of bat-shaped kite.

designed to give expression to different subject matters such
as all sorts of objects, characters and geometric figures.

Tile kite, commonly called "seat curtain," needs only
three bamboo strips to make a framework. Two are crossly
placed on a square paper and the third is made in the shape
of a bow and placed across the top. At the tail of the frame,
three paper tapes are attached. Tile kite is the most ordinary
self-made kite among the people.

From the dynasties of Tang and Song, Chinese kites started
to spread to the outer world, first to Korea, Japan, Malaysia
and then to America and Europe, where influenced by the
industrial revolution in Europe, Chinese kites developed
towards aircrafts. In the NASA Museum in Washington, US,
there is a sign conspicuously stated that the earliest aircrafts
were China's kites and rockets.


# Puppet


Puppet made its appearance for the first time in the Spring
and Autumn Period. In 1979, a puppet was unearthed
from a Han Dynasty tomb in Laixi of Shandong Province.
The puppet, 193 centimeters in height and composed of
thirteen articulated parts, can be made to sit, stand or kneel.
The discovery indicates that the function of puppets at that
time had shifted from being a funerary object to a thing for

entertainment, which foretold the birth of puppet show.

In the classic writing *Tong dian* (Laws and Rules Recorded) written by Du You of the Tang Dynasty, there is a short passage which goes, "In the last years of Han Dynasty, puppets started to perform for entertainment on grand occasions. In earlier times, they were used only at funerals." By the Sui Dynasty, the embryonic form of puppet show had taken shape. Even scenes from traditional opera could be performed with puppets. From the Tang Dynasty, puppetry grew to mature day by day. The murals and poems of the prosperous period of Tang Dynasty stored in Cave No. 31 of Mogao Grottos in Dunhuang, Gansu Province indicate that different categories of puppets including glove puppets, marionettes and rod-hand puppets had already appeared.

The puppet show came to its prime in the dynasties of Song and Yuan. Puppet show troupes mushroomed in Song Dynasty, offering performances of various subject matters. From Yuan Dynasty, puppets could be manipulated to act vividly the gamut of human emotions – happiness, anger, grief and joy.

From the Ming down to the Qing Dynasty, diversified schools of puppet show spread all over the country, each with local flavor of its own. Take the marionette show in Quanzhou of Fujian Province for an example. Not only was the music accompaniment excellent, but also were the puppets exquisitely made and manipulated with superb skills. A single puppet figure could be controlled by as many as twenty up to thirty strings. In Qing Dynasty, rod puppet show prevailed among which the Beijing rod puppet show was played in the royal court as a special-form Peking opera.

By traditional puppet making craft, the head and limbs of puppet figures were made of camphorwood, which is sweet smelling, anti-worm-eaten, hardly out of shape, and lustrous after polishing. In general some a dozen steps are needed in the working procedure including material choosing, rough carving, meticulous carving, papering, polishing, coating with clay, applying powder, putting on facial makeup and coating with lacquer. The puppet show features local characteristics in that even in the same region, the manipulating skill, figures designed and stage art may be entirely different.

Performance of marionette show at Heyang, Shaanxi.

Rod puppet Jiaozan, head high 17.5 cm. Jiao is a valiant general in traditional puppet drama, Jinxian, Hebei.

Of different varieties of puppet show, the rod puppet show is the most popular. The rod puppet show falls into three types: large-sized, medium-sized and small-sized according to performing style and figure designs. The small-sized puppets, also known as refined puppets, about 40 centimeters in length, are exquisite, precise in movements and adept at playing both civil and martial roles. Large-sized puppets are 1.4 meters long, five kilos heavy, can play putting on clothes, lighting a fire, kowtowing, wielding a sword, etc. The puppets of the statue similar to a human being often perform together with "human puppets" played by kids, in a bid to have an artistic effect of "mixing the false with the real" and "false and true at the same time." The rod puppets are worked by a "life-rod" connecting the puppet head and two "hand rods" joining the hands of the puppet. The puppet is ingeniously designed and manipulated so that its eyes and mouth are movable.

Glove puppets, also called "palm puppets," are worked by fitting on the hand of the performer. The glove puppet show is most prevalent in Quanzhou of Fujian Province. The puppet is about 30 centimeters in length, consisting of a head, a trunk and clothes. The head is made of camphorwood with gears installed to control the movement of eyes and mouth. The performer's index finger is used to manipulate the puppet head, the middle finger and the thumb the two puppet hands respectively. The glove puppet show is characterized by various movements, both precise and nimble including movements that require superior skills such as unfolding a fan, changing clothes, performing sword-dance, fighting with a weapon, jumping through a window, etc.

A marionette is a jointed puppet moved by strings. It is composed of the head, the trunk, limbs and manipulating strings, some sixty centimeters in length. Its head is carved out of camphorwood, Chinese linden or willow wood, with gears to control facial expressions. Hands are of two types: the martial type and the civil type. The martial-type hands are manipulated to wield spear and cudgels; the civil type wave fans or raise wine cups. The puppet feet can be bare, booted, or in the shape of female's.

The iron wire puppet show circulated in the western Fujian and eastern Guangdong region, took shape in the last days of Qing Dynasty and enjoyed popularity for a period of time. The most distinct feature is that it maintains the manipulating

Puppets in the glove puppet show *A Journey to the West*. The figures measure 28 cm in height, Zhangzhou, Fujian.

123

Marionettes Zhang
Fei, Liu Bei, Guan
Yu, 80 cm high,
Zhangzhou, Fujian.

skills of the shadow play. The operators working in a transparent case, using iron wire to accomplish each movement. The manipulating rod is called iron branch. The puppet is one to one and a half meters in length made of paulownia wood, with paper hands and wooden feet. The head is made of red clay, baked and then coated with waterproof coloring. Different types of facial make-up indicating personalities and characters are applied. The operators, sitting or standing, manipulate the puppet from behind.

## Silhouette

Shadow play is a popular folk opera belonging in the category of puppy show in which performers use leather or cardboard silhouettes to enact plays. A light is shone onto a screen, behind which performers operate the silhouettes while singing to the company of music. It is a form of art unique to China where folk arts and crafts are ingeniously

combined with theatrical performance,

Silhouettes are similar to paper-cuts, but differ in that the hands and legs are joined with string so that they are movable. The silhouette figures were cut from cardboard at first and from donkey hide or ox-hide, sheep-hide, etc. later on. Usually a piece of hide is cut, colored, ironed and joined into a figure with nimble limbs. The tools used in making silhouette figures are rather particular about, which include five categories: knives, blades, files, drills, and prods, for shaping the head, trunk, legs, hands and feet respectively.

The silhouette figures, vivid in shape and rich in color, are projected onto a screen. In a performance, the operator, while singing to the accompaniment of music, manipulates the figures as the story of the play requires. To adapt to the form of screen expression, the skill of combining abstractness and reality is applied in shadow play in which scenes are made artistic, exaggerate and dramatic. Aside from screen presentation, silhouette figures can be played with hands for personal amusement, or placed on window sills as ornaments. They can be appreciated or kept as collectables.

Shadow play can be traced back to the Western Han Dynasty. Legend has it that in the reign of Emperor Wen (203-157 B.C.), a court lady who was playing with the crown prince in front of the window, had human figures cut from Chinese parasol leaves, which she managed to reflect on the gauze windows for fun. That is the origin of shadow play. Actually shadow play in China started from the Northern Song Dynasty and gradually prospered. According to *Dream of the Eastern Capital* written by Meng Yuanlao in Song Dynasty, in the capital of the Northern Song Dynasty, places of entertainment increased rapidly in number where shadow play started as a genre of folk art form among ballad-singing, comic dialogue, story-telling with drum accompaniment etc. In the capital city of Lin'an (now Hangzhou), a shadow play troupe named "Painted-Leather Society" was established. In the third year of Zhengde under the reign of Emperor Renzong in the Ming Dynasty, a hundred-drama festival was held in Beijing in which performances were also given by shadow play operators. In the Qing Dynasty, shadow play further developed and became popular, with more items on

Silhouette in Eastern Route shadow play of Shaanxi in late-Ming Dynasty.

the program to choose from, more varieties of figures, and more meticulous in the carving skills. During the reign of Emperor Jiaqing (1786-1820), the shadow play troupes also gave performances for home celebration on New Year Day and other festivals. At that time, quite a few Peking opera actors joined in the performance of shadow play. Since the mid-Qing Dynasty, types of facial makeup such as *sheng* (male role), *dan* (female role), *jing* (painted-face role), *mo* (elderly male role) and *chou* (role of clown) appeared in shadow play, as learned from Peking Opera.

The shadow play is commonly seen in rural areas in North China and the provinces of Sichuan, Hu'nan and Hubei, where different local schools were formed each with rich local flavor of their own among which some outstanding ones are the Shaanxi shadow, Tangshan shadow and Longdong shadow.

Beijing Western School shadow play in the early years of Qing Dynasty. Traits of different figures are emphatically depicted with meticulous carving.

The shadow play in Shaanxi is plain and simple in figure shape, exquisite in workmanship and very decorative. It is subdivided into two factions: the eastern route and the western route. The eastern route silhouette figures are small in statue, characterized by delicacy and ingenuity, whereas the western route ones force and plainness.

The Tangshan shadow play is one of the important branches in which the figures are carved from donkey hide and separated into six parts joined with iron wire and silk thread so that they are easy to be turned round. Besides, as three sticks are fixed on each figure, the puppet can be made to move deftly like people in real life.

The Gansu Longdong shadow play became popular as early as the dynasties of Ming and Qing. Its figures appear exaggerated with a large head and a small trunk, upper half narrower than the lower, arms reaching down over knees. The coloring of facial make-up is basically the same as that of Shaanxi opera, that is, black color symbolizing loyalty, white treachery, red upright, painted bravery, blank honesty. Other properties such as tables, beds, animals, plants, etc are made a bit vague so as to make the chief figures prominent. In preparing silhouette figures the hide of young black ox is

Qing-dynasty shadow play: *Prince White Dragon.*

Qing-dynasty Shaanxi Eastern Route shadow play *Fengyi Pavilion* is extremely exquisite with the richly ornamented arbors, pavilions, terraces, etc.

chosen as material. First draw a draft on the hide, and then carve with different types of cutting tools, and then color with transparent coloring agents which are not blended. The last step is ironing, which is the most important as well as difficult part. The silhouette figures so prepared, when dried in the air, can be arranged for performance on the stage.

Shadow play *The Story of White Snake* in Qing Dynasty, Tangshan, Hebei.

# Arts and Crafts in the Field of Commerce

# Shop Sign

Inscriptions often appear on wine-shop streamers.

In China, shop signs are of two major categories: one is signboard on which the name of the shop is given; the other is trade sign, giving the line of business. The sign board is usually in the shape of an oblong wooden board and the trade sign often gives the commodity to be sold or items or services by means of images.

Not until the Song Dynasty, shop signs were used chiefly in restaurants and teahouses, and then drugstores, draperies, pawnshops, medicated plaster shops, hotels, tobacconists, etc. started to have a piece of cloth hanging in front of the door showing trade signs. The masterpiece *Pure Brightness Day on the River* displays a prosperous and noisy scene of the streets in the capital, with rows and rows of stores carrying shop signs of various types clearly seen.

When it came to the Ming and Qing dynasties, shop signs became numerous in variety following the blooming of market-place commerce, which fall largely into four categories: image sign, written sign, material object sign and symbol sign.

The image sign refers to the models of the commodities sold in the shop. In a tobacconist, an enlarged tobacco leaf and a tobacco pouch were drawn on a piece of cloth or a wooden board; in a shoe store, a model of the sole of a shoe was hanging up.

In written signs words were written or engraved as shop sign. Generally there were single-type sign and compound-type sign. The single sign was simple and clear at a glance, such as a big character "pawn" indicating a pawn shop, and a character "pickle" referring to a sauce and pickle shop. The compound-type sign gave first place to figures accompanied by corresponding words. For example, in the Chongwenmen Street in Beijing in the last years of the Qing Dynasty, shops dealing in oil baskets, real oil baskets were hung up as sign, with a big character "oil" written on the basket. The signboard was usually made of wood, in the shape of rectangle, square or bottle gourd, coated with black lacquer on both sides, sometimes covered with gold foil to make it more conspicuous.

The real object sign refers to the sample goods hung at the door of a shop, such as worsted of all colors, leg wrappings, odd bits of cloth, etc. to denote a draper's.

The symbol sign was originally a token of the shop, something like the present-day logo, which was accepted by the public in the passage of years and became the sign of the shop.

The shop signs ware made chiefly from paper, cloth, leather, bamboo, wood, aluminum, iron, and copper and tin, chosen according to the nature of the commodity, and the scope and features of the business. Its technological process includes wood carving, embroidery, iron sheet galvanizing, weaving, etc. Traditional Chinese calligraphy, painting, real object model, etc. are often used in designing shop signs to give a rich folk flavor and unique national style. Different nationalities tend to use the totem they worship for major patterns on the signboard. For instance, as the Han people set a great store by dragon, the horizontal bar of the sign board is often carved in the shape of a dragon.

Shop sign of Neiliansheng Shoe Store opened in the reign of Emperor Xianfeng in Qing Dynasty. The sign is made of wooden board, bearing the name of the shop and a drawing of a boot and a shoe.

The art of the layout and decorations in shop signs calls for symmetry. Therefore, signs are usually placed on either side of the shop to give a perceptive effect of balance. To better bring play to publicity, signs are displayed in different forms, some fixed on a stone base, some hung under the eaves, some written or drawn on the wall, doorpost or lintel of a door, and some sticking out to the street with a long pole. In coloring, red, yellow, blue, black, and white are most popular, in particular red or yellow, which symbolizes auspiciousness and jubilation. In decorative patterns, coin, dragon, cloud, the character *fu* (blessings), etc. representing propitiousness and wealth are preferred. In addition, the cross bar on which shop sign is hanging is often made into the shape of dragon or bat to symbolize "soaring like a holy dragon" or "good luck descending upon the house."

Signboard of worsted shop using lamp-shaped signs composed of interlocked worsted rings.

Merchants in traditional Chinese society mostly hold in awe the God of Wealth and founders of their business. The reverence for their shrines, statues and spirit tablets is in time extended to the shop signs. In the eye of the merchants, shop signs are symbols of "treasures coming into the house," and

131

Beijing Wang Mazi scissors shop of Qing Dynasty.

"fortune rolling in." There are various taboos in the use of shop signs. For example, the shop signs are not "hung up" but "invited," because the character *gua* (hang up) is believed to be unlucky. Similarly, the falling of shop signs on the ground is also considered unlucky, because the God of Wealth might be offended even by such a petty thing. From this, we can see the folk ways and social conventions behind the traditional handicrafts.

# Packaging

Packaging is closely related to people's daily life. Traditionally the guidelines on packaging in China are always "for the convenience of the users" and "pleasing to the eyes."

In earlier days, natural materials were used in packing such as tree leaves, bamboo, lotus leaves, palm leaves, gourds, cocoanut shells, shells of shellfish, animal skin, etc. Later on, man-made material were used including fabrics, ceramics, metals, lacquer ware, woodware, jadeware, paper, etc. As early as the late years of the primitive society, packaging had already started. Bamboo tubes, gourd shells, cocoanut shells, earthen jugs, etc. were used to hold liquids; baskets made from bamboo or willow twigs, were used to hold solid objects. Sometimes commodities were directed wrapped in bamboo leaves, lotus leaves, etc. In China materials, ornaments and styles in packaging differ in different historical periods, changing with the productivity, and scientific and technological development, and conforming to the fashion of the time.

Shang-dynasty jade dagger-axe treasured in Palace Museum. The silk and hemp fabric packaging closely adhered to the surface owing to the passage of time.

The pottery wares emerged in the Neolithic Age was the first great invention of man-made packaging materials. In comparison with natural materials, they have the advantages of being durable, antiseptic, and anti-worm-eaten. They also excel in long-distance transportation and in being various in forms. It is interesting that the earliest food cans were discovered in China – the twelve airtight food cans unearthed in Baoshan of Hubei in 316 B.C. These cans were tightly sealed with multi-layer materials such as straw mats, bamboo leaves, wet clay, etc. Individual cans were cased with bamboo baskets having a handle above for convenient carrying. On the outmost layer, silk was covered before they were tied up with thin bamboo strips or silk ribbon, which were sealed with clay, attached with label bearing the description of the food contained in the can. By this process the food can be kept for a long period of time without going bad or discoloring.

In the Shang and Zhou dynasties, traders started to appear. At that time, bronze vessels were commonly used as packaging material to hold alcoholic drinks, meat, etc. Other packaging materials included earthenware, lacquer ware, wooden articles, leather utensils, bamboo articles, etc. which were also used as containers. The remnants of silk wrappings round the Shang-dynasty jade dagger-axe housed in the Palace Museum in Beijing are tightly adhered to its surface with the passage of time.

In the Spring and Autumn and Warring States Period, trade became more flourishing. In order to attract customers, some traders laid special stress on the packaging of commodities. The ever-increasingly exquisite packaging sometimes caused the secondary to supersede the primary. An ancient Chinese fable entitled *Selling the Casket without the Pearls* is included in the classic *Han Fei Tzu*. It is about a native of the state of Chu selling pearls in the State of Zheng. He had a casket made of rare wood, scented it with spices, inlaid it with jade and other precious jewels. The result was that the

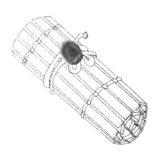

Han-dynasty lute housed in Palace Museum. Lute here refers to dried clay with stamps on it, used for sealing bamboo-slip letters.

men of Zheng were eager to buy the casket, but returned the pearls to him.

Paper is the second significant invention with respect to man-made packaging materials. Before Cai Lun (?-121) made what was to be termed as paper in the Eastern Han Dynasty, ancient paper on which map was drawn already appeared in the Qin and Han dynasties. By the Western Han Dynasty bronze mirrors were wrapped with rough paper made from bamboo and hemp fibers. Improved paper was soon used in packaging articles of everyday use, food, medicine, etc.

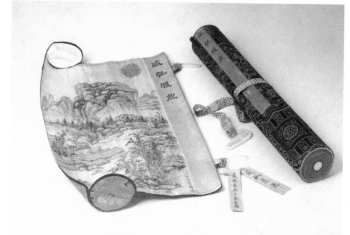

Qing-dynasty brocade: case of scroll painting *Wei Hu Huo Lu* (a painting depicting Emperor Qianlong hunting deer at Chengde Summer Resort), 36 cm long, 6.5 in diameter, housed in Palace Museum.

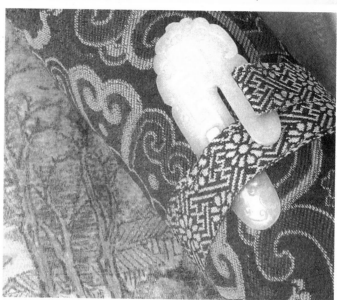

Scroll painting case (partial).

Henceforth paper has become the most common and important packaging material. In the Tang tombs in Astana, Xinjiang, a traditional Chinese medicine called "weirui" pill wrapped in a small piece of square white hemp paper was unearthed, on which are the words "taking 15 pills each time on an empty stomach before going to bed." When printing was invented in the Song Dynasty, the technique of package printing was developed and applied to practice. The combination of paper making and printing, in addition to the application of traditional Chinese culture and arts such as poetry, painting, calligraphy and seal-engraving, made traditional packaging manifest rich national flavor in decoration and external appearance. Besides, following the development of lacquer craft, lacquer vessels used as packaging material were prevailing in the Han Dynasty and have since been used through the ages as a major packaging material.

In the Sui, Tang and Song dynasties, Chinese economy remained stable and thriving; cultural and economic exchanges with foreign countries occurred frequently. Exotic cultural impact often reflected on commodity packages. Take the then more flourished ceramic crafts for an example. Quite a number of ceramic utensils were distinctive in shape, refined in designs, of which some bearing the local flavor of the Western Region. When earthen and china cups, bottles, jugs, etc. were used to hold wine or vinegar, customers often attracted by the tasteful packages. Even the wine and vinegar contained in the vessels were benefited from it and had a rise in selling price. On the outer packages of some commodities, places of production, the name of shops were

Qing-dynasty Pu'er tea lump-shaped five-kid package: It is a large parcel containing five small tea bags wrapped with indocalamus leaves, a local packaging method continued to be used today.

*135*

Jingdezhen china bowl wrapped with straw rope.

marked so as not only to ensure genuine goods at a fair price, but also prevent fake quality commodities from passing off.

In the Ming and Qing dynasties, with the budding of capitalism, people's commodity consciousness intensified, as manifested in commodity packaging where all sorts of lacquer cases and silk cases used for packaging became more and more elegant and sumptuous. Packaging itself seemed to become a form of art in which the most typical was the packaging of articles for the use of the royal court in the Qing Dynasty. Actually such were specially manufactured, some by the imperial workshops and some by folk craftspeople. The former embodies typical royal style and characteristics of the times in material choosing, designing and ornaments whereas the latter gives expression to practical use, with ornaments that are designed to fit the taste of the imperial family. Needless to say, the materials used in the royal workshops are largely red sandlewood, lacquer ware, enamel, bamboo carvings, sold and silver inlaid vessels, silk fabrics, etc., and the decoration procedures include carving, engraving on gold and silver, painting, inlaying, baking, weaving, etc., showing the superb skills of the Qing-dynasty arts and crafts.

# Legends concerning Traditional Arts and Crafts of China

In the ancient times, the Chinese people held that all sorts of articles used in daily life and production were the creations of sages. The *Kao Gong Ji* left from the pre-Qin period raised distinctively the plain doctrine of sages' creation of articles: "Sages create articles and skillful people state them and observe them. They are called handicraftsmen. All things related to handicrafts are done by sages." According to the handicraft legends that have passed down from generation to generation, the right of earliest handicraft invention often belonged to those sages with deities' means or saints' ways, such as tribal chieftains, emperors and queens or their subjects. That is why there are a series of legends about how sages created articles and those very intelligent sages became the earliest handicraftsmen. For instances, Emperor Xuanyuan (Yellow Emperor, a legendary ruler of China in remote antiquity) invented armor and helmet, boat and vehicle, hat and crown, and clothing; Youchaoshi built nests with timbers and initiated rooms and houses; Emperor Xuanyuan's wife Leizu was worshiped as goddess of silkworms as she taught women of her time to pluck mulberry leaves and feed silkworms; Fuxishi invented fishnet and the *qin* (a seven-stringed plucked musical instrument) and *se* (a twenty-five stringed plucked instrument); Emperor Yan invented the *lei* (ploughs) and *si* (plowshares); Zhou Gong invented the *zhinan che* (a vehicle pointing south); Meng Tian of the Qin Dynasty invented writing brush; and Cai Lun of the Han Dynasty invented paper-making, etc.

Most of the earliest legends about handicrafts initially circulated verbally among artisans of the same trade and was then expanded to the society. During the circulation passing down from generation to generation, the legends were continuously enriched and perfected, becoming beautiful and touching. They were either about the origin of the different trades and their unique characteristics, or about the earliest master artisans who started the trade, or about how craftsmen faced bravely hard life and miserable sufferings. It may be said in a certain sense that the legends about handicrafts are used to sing and praise those skillful craftsmen and artisans little known in the past ages.

The legends about handicrafts were inherited not only orally. Part of earlier legends was also recorded in ancient books. The content of this part was rather stable but due to continuous supplement and farfetched interpretation, it has been gradually divorced from its original historical record and taken on a new legendry look.

The miraculous puppet made by artisan Yanshi greatly surprised King Mu of the Zhou Dynasty.

# Yanshi and His Puppets

In the Western Zhou Dynasty when King Mu was on the throne there was an artisan named Yanshi. The puppet he made bore strong resemblance to a living person. At first, King Mu thought the puppet was only Yanshi's attendant. When Yanshi gave orders for him to advance, retreat, bend forward or backward, it responded with no difference from a being. When opening its jaws, it could drawl out a song; and when moving its arms, it could sway and move about as in a dance. When the performance came to an end, the puppet cast seductive eyes to King Mu's concubine in high favor. King Mu flew into a great rage, firmly believing the puppet, dexterous and quick in action, must be a real being instead of a puppet and wanted to put Yanshi to death on the spot. Yanshi immediately disassembled the puppet to show that the puppet was made of no more than leather, wood, gum and lacquer, and black, white, red and blue pigments. King Mu hastened forward and examined carefully, finding the puppet had all visceral organs available while for the exterior, muscles and bones, joints, skin, hair, and teeth were also all available with nothing missing. However, they were all man-made things. When they were assembled together, it became a living puppet again. King Mu gasped in admiration of Yanshi's superb skill, very pleased and sincerely convinced.

# Lu Ban, a Carpenter Consecrated by Artisans of All Crafts

Lu Ban, also known as Gongshu Ban, was a renowned carpenter of the Lu State during the Spring and Autumn Period and the Warring States Period. The social changes made artisans gain some freedom and the wide use of ironware provided favorable conditions for the development of handicraft technology. In the respect of tool innovation and workmanship, Lu Ban found his own way to distinction. Ancient books recorded his deeds in tool innovation and fabrication of various kinds of utensils for daily use, such as the *yinkuo* (an appliance used for straightening out lumber) and shovel. Lu Ban was originally a carpenter but it had already been said in the ancient times of China that he was also engaged in other workmanships, such as coppersmith, stonemason, etc. According to the legend circulated in the Han Dynasty, Lu Ban was said to carve and paint the crossbeams of the palace in Luoyang and build a bridge in the vicinity of Chang'an. Afterwards, this kind of legend increased day by day at various places and people took not too much notice whether these legends were in conformity with Gongshu Ban's history during the Warring States Period but instead they took Lu Ban as an ideal character of skilled artisan. For uplifting the notability of their respective trade, many trades such as carpenter, bricklayer, stonemason, shipbuilder, vehicle fabricator, etc. all consecrated Lu Ban as the founder of their respective trade. As a result, the phenomenon "artisans of all crafts consecrate Lu Ban" occurred.

# The Legend of Ganjiang and Moye

During the Spring and Autumn Period and the Warring States, the iron abounding in the Yue State was the best in quality and sword-making masters emerged in large numbers, of whom Ganjiang was a man of great reputation. Afterwards, Ganjiang went to the Wu State and was tied in wedlock with Moye. As He Lü, the king of the Wu State, was fond of double-edged sword, the two of them were appointed to an official position. For casting an excellent sword, the king of the Wu State sent someone to acquire the best iron from the Yue State and ordered Ganjiang to work out a unique sword within three months or he would be beheaded for disobeying the order. Ganjiang and Moye went on working hard night and day for two months, but the iron was still not melted in the furnace. The deadline for the sword was due soon but they were at their wits' end. Ganjiang brought up the story about how his master worker and his wife jumped into the furnace so that the iron was melted and a good sword was worked out within the deadline set by the king of the Yue State. After hearing the story, Moye decided to sacrifice her life for the sword. After turning the issue over in his mind for a long time, Ganjiang said as hair and nails of human beings were parents' essence, maybe they could melt the iron. So Moye cut off her long hair and nails and threw them into the blazing fire. Simultaneously, three hundred young boys and girls did all they could to air-blast the furnace with more

The couple of Ganjiang and Moye, masters of sword casting, tempered double-edged swords in blazing fire day and night.

carbon added in the blazing fire. In an instant the iron melted and a couple of unique "male and female swords" in the world was finally wrought. The male sword, covering with lines in tortoise-shell pattern on the surface, was named Ganjiang while the female sword, covering with lines in water-wave pattern on the surface, was named Moye.

However, the legend had several different versions. In the *Wu Di Ji* (A Record of the Wu State), the swords were not wrought until Moye jumped into the furnace. The *Lie Yi Zhuan* (Stories of Supernatural Beings) and the *Shou Shen Ji* (Stories of Searching for Deities) even arranged an offspring for Ganjiang and Moye to show artisans' strength through complicated plot of vengeance. Ganjiang offered the king of the Wu State only the female sword and concealed the male sword for himself. When finding the truth, the king of the Wu State put Ganjiang to death. When growing up, Ganjiang and Moye's son Mei Jian Chi tried to avenge his parents but the king of the Wu State was on strict guard of assassination. Thanks to the help of a swordsman who promised to avenge him, Mei Jian Chi handed the male sword to the swordsman and then committed suicide by cutting his own throat. Under the plea of offering the male sword and Mei Jian Chi's head, the swordsman succeeded to access the king and finally perished together with the king of the Wu State.

## The Legend of Brother Kilns

The Longquan celadon is one of the notable varieties of the traditional ceramics of China. This legend was about how two brothers, Zhang Shengyi and Zhang Sheng'er, of Longquan County, Zhejiang, in the Southern Song Dynasty improved celadon. The legend has it that the Zhang family was engaged in porcelain-making from generation to generation. According to their father's last wish, the two brothers ran their respective kiln and tried hard to make innovation. Beginning with colors, Zhang Sheng'er analyzed seriously all the colors man could see in the sky and on the earth and came to the conclusion that cyan was the basis of all colors, the essence of all colors and the most beautiful color, as it pleased both the eye and the mind. After discussion, the two brothers decided to take cyan as the fixed color of the Zhang family to make porcelain. When he happened to see a green plum tree standing gracefully erect by the kiln shed, Zhang Sheng'er thought the cyan of plums was the most beautiful cyan. Plucking the plum leaves together with small plums, he had them simmered into thick juice, blended it into glaze and applied it onto the porcelain base. Finally celadon, which was bluish, came into being and caused a great sensation. After seeing it, Emperor Gaozong

(1127-1131) of the Southern Song Dynasty was so delighted with it that he could hardly bear to put it down on seeing it and issued the imperial decree to change the porcelain kiln of Zhang Sheng'er into a government-run porcelain industry and conferred the title of the "Diyao Kiln" (The Younger Brother's Kiln) upon it.

Zhang Shengyi also cherished high ambitions in his life, trying to burn out a kind of crackle porcelain, which had always been believed to be something bestowed by deities, as an artifact. In order to disclose the secret of porcelain crackling, he kept to himself and never got married. After serious studies and investigations, he found that for gaining a few pieces of crackle porcelain the people of his time often threw a living person into the blazing kiln. The blood and moisture of the living person caused the crackling of the porcelain. When blood congealed, the color was purple. That is why the color of crackle porcelain was always of a little blood red. Besides, when the porcelain base came across moisture, there was no time for it to shrink and hence crackling in polygonal shape. As Longquan was available with a special kind of clay with the color of a little blood red, the key issue was moisture and the right amount of water injection. Zhang Shengyi persisted in doing contrast test but failed again and again. Once in a severe winter, when taking a bowl of noodle to him for eating, his brother's wife Wu Zhenzhen found him injecting water into the kiln. It came naturally to her that her brother-in-law was trying to put out the fire in the kiln, so she lent him a hand. Unexpectedly, a kiln of crackle celadon full of fish-scale cracks came out, seeming cracked but not broken. Indescribably wonderful crackle porcelain! Zhang Shengyi's crackle celadon created a sensation of the court above and the masses below. Immediately his kiln was decided to be one of the five famous kilns of the Song Dynasty and its products were exclusively for the use in the imperial palace and export. As Zhang Shengyi was the elder brother of the two brothers, his crackle celadon was also named the "Geyao Kiln" (The Elder Brother's Kiln) celadon.

The two brothers, Zhang Shengyi and Zhang Sheng'er, worked hard to improve celadon technology.

## Origin of Kesi Silk

The *kesi* silk is a variety of Chinese silk weaving, complicated in workmanship but rich in expression. When the troops of Jin Dynasty went south to invade the Song Dynasty, a youngster named Qiaosheng at Likou, Suzhou, lived on weaving *juan* (a kind of thin and tough silk) but due to the chaos caused by the war he had to change his occupation to trade shreds with sweets. Once from the rags he traded with sweets he found a piece of shred with the same flower-and-bird pattern on the reverse and the obverse sides, looking neither like brocade nor like embroidery, and the pattern was very soft and pleasing to the eye. He decided to learn this kind of workmanship. One day by a lotus pond Qiaosheng helped a girl fish up the clothes washed away by the water. For expressing her thanks, the girl gave him a lotus seed. On returning home, he put the lotus seed into a vat and it began to put forth lotus flowers of various colors. All of a sudden, he found the girl in the lotus vat weaving silk cloth stealthily. The girl wrung juice out of the lotus flowers and lotus leaves she had gathered and dyed the fibers of the lotus root into different brilliant colors. Then she made little and dainty shuttles one after another with pointed bamboo leaves. She loaded the lotus fibers of different colors, from light-colored to deep-colored, into the shuttles and arranged them in alignment in front of the loom. The fiber of the lotus root in the shuttles became silk fiber. She changed the shuttles one after another, weaving in a very meticulous way. Qiaosheng was so surprised that he jumped out from behind the door. Knowing that her secret was discovered, the girl stayed at Qiaosheng's home and passed on her skill to him. They named this kind of weaving method "hesi," meaning the silk woven jointly by them. As the people of Suzhou pronounced the word "he" as "ke," people called it "kesi silk" afterwards.

## Gourd-shaped Porcelain Canteen and the Yue's Troops

At the end of the Southern Song Dynasty, there was a kiln artisan named Hulu at the Cizhouyao Kiln. He was clever and skillful. Once he made a kind of porcelain canteen, thick at both ends but thin in the center, convenient to carry. As it looked exactly like the gourd used by immortals in the legend, people called it porcelain gourd, also known as the canteen of the Yue's troops. The legend goes that for recovering the occupied territory in the north, Marshal Yue Fei fought with his army from the Yangtze River all the way to the Mt. Taihang.

The kiln artisans of the Cizhouyao Kiln were very excited and tried to present the Yue's troops with a kind of porcelain canteen in kidney shape for them to carry conveniently on the march. The kiln artisan Hulu thought he should send Marshal Yue and his troops a precious canteen just like that used by Taishang Laojun (the Very High Lord in the legend) to hold elixir vitae as Marshal Yue had rendered outstanding service to the Song Dynasty. It was said that the water used to blend the clay for making the treasured canteen of the Very High Lord was taken from nine rivers and eighteen lakes. So he sent someone to take the spring water from nine springs, such as the Black Dragon Spring, the Yellow Dragon Spring, the Dark-green Dragon Spring, the Old Dragon Spring, the Jade Dragon Spring, etc. In the clay to make the canteen, he added costly medicines, such as musk, glossy ganoderma, bezoar, peppermint, etc. Finally, when the canteen was done to hold water or wine, not only could it quench thirst and relieve summer heat but also cure all diseases.

Artisans of Cizhouyao Kiln presented porcelain canteen to Yue Fei.

The officers and men of the Yue's troops went on with the march with the porcelain canteen, sweeping northward from victory to victory. Afterwards due to the collusion between Qin Hui and the Jin troops, the Yue's troops were besieged on the top of the Mt. Jiushi. Before long all the water bottled in the ordinary porcelain canteen was drunk up but the officers and men found to the surprise that the water and wine in Marshal Yuan's porcelain canteen would never go empty. They found some big Chinese characters "Porcelain Canteen with Water from Nine Springs" and some small Chinese characters "Cizhouyao Kiln" inscribed at the bottom of the canteen. The officers and men drank freely with great joviality. After drinking the wine to their heart's content, they rushed down the mountain. Afterwards, the Yue's troops recovered a large stretch of territory.

# Qiu Changchun, the Forefather of Jade Carving in Beijing

Qiu Chuji, also known as Taoist Changchun, was the earliest ancestor of jade trade in Beijing and was called Ancestor Qiu by artisans. At the end of the Southern Song Dynasty, Ancestor Qiu was born in a town in Shangdong and his family financial situation was poverty-stricken. Not far away from his home, there was a small jade workshop, where he acknowledged somebody as his master and learned

Qiu Changchun studied intensively how to perfect jade-carving technology.

the skills of jade carving. Due to this father's early death of illness, Ancestor Qiu discontinued his apprenticeship. Later, during the chaos caused by war, he could live on nothing but to make a living on carrying people across the river on his back. At the riverside he happened to meet a Taoist priest. On seeing that the young man was intelligent by natural endowments, the Taoist priest accepted him as a disciple and let him roam everywhere to study jadeware as his main job so that he could learn skills and help the distressed. Afterwards, Ancestor Qiu had the opportunity to tour around China to those places rich in jade, such as Xinjiang. He learned the skill of how to look at a piece of jade and judge its worth. Besides, he also studied hard to master various kinds of workmanship for artisans.

After the Yuan Dynasty founded its capital in Beijing, Ancestor Qiu came all the way to Beijing through the northwest and settled down at the Baiyun Guan (The White Cloud Taoist Temple) to devote himself to jadeware fabrication. His nationwide touring widened his field of vision. By drawing on other people's merits and making use of the knowledge passed on to him by the Taoist priest, every piece of jadeware he fabricated was exquisite. Not only was Ancestor Qiu proficient in jadeware himself, he also passed on his jade carving skills to others in accordance with their aptitude. With his advocate and support, the jadeware trade came into being in Beijing and the Baiyun Guan became an institute for Ancestor Qiu to pass on his skills.

# Gong Chun Teapot and Lotus-and-toad Teapot

Yixing, Jiangsu, is known as the "pottery capital with a history of one thousand years" and the fame of the *zisha* (purple-clay) teapot of Yixing has spread even throughout the country. If someone asks who made the greatest contribution to the *zisha* teapot craft, all the local people would unanimously give the credit to Gong Chun and told about the story of the Gong Chun teapot and the lotus-and-toad teapot he had made.

By the Ming Dynasty, the pottery-making industry of Yixing had already reached a fairly large scale. At Yixing there was a farmer surnamed Gong and his only son was named Gong Chun. From childhood, Gong Chun liked to watch his neighbor, an old monk, make pottery. But as the old monk was afraid of losing his own way of living in case of passing on his skills to the boy, he was unwilling to teach the boy his pottery workmanship. So Gong Chun could do nothing but study intensively by himself. One night, when he saw the unconventional shadow on the knot of a peach tree cast by the moon, he got an inspiration to make a *zisha* teapot with the peach tree knot as the teapot body. As the shape of the teapot was natural and innate, it was simple and unsophisticated, bringing about a new *zisha* handicraft, and the people named this craft Gong Chun teapot after its initiator. The greedy magistrate of the local prefecture asked Gong Chun to make a teapot for him. Gong Chun hated to fawn on and flatter influential officials but this time he made an exception to promise him. Finally, he made a lotus-and-toad teapot with the magistrate as the model. The toad opening its big month was the very image of the magistrate. This lotus-and-toad teapot was not only a masterpiece of the *zisha* teapot but also a scathing satire on those influential officials avaricious of wealth.

## The Beauty Offered for Sacrifice

This is a legend about a famous variety of porcelain named "ji hong" (the red for sacrifice). The color of "ji hong" is sleek and glossy, stable and not flowing. It is the top-grade porcelain of red glaze and the most precious one was produced in the Ming Dynasty.

The legend goes that in the Ming Dynasty, the royal porcelain plant in Jingdezhen got an imperial edict to make a special kind of porcelain. In case of failure within the deadline, the punishment would be death penalty. As the kiln could not reach the temperature needed, the old pottery artisan in charge failed again and again. He sighed and groaned at home and his daughter worried very much for her father.

On the following day at noon time, the old artisan's daughter, all dressed up, sent lunch to the plant for her father. As the temperature in the kiln was still not high enough, all the people present were too sorrowful to eat anything. All of a sudden, the artisan's daughter shouted, pushed aside the people around her, and jumped into the kiln. Just at the time when everybody was crying and yelling, the temperature in the kiln went up and the porcelain required was made. As the old artisan's daughter saved everybody, the later generations call this kind of porcelain "the beauty offered for sacrifice."

## Legend about Ceramics with Multicolored Glaze

This legend is about a story of the return of a prodigal. The legend has it that an artisan proficient at porcelain craft named Zhao Dacheng at the Cizhouyao Kiln in Pengcheng Town had two sons. The first son Zhao Dechang was not only kind-hearted but also extremely skillful in handicraft while the second son Zhao

Debao was, just on the contrary, gluttonous and lazy, unwilling to learn any skill. After dividing up the family property and living apart, the good-hearted elder brother gave the better kiln to his brother and took a worse one for himself. However, due to the superb porcelain technology he had learned from his father and his diligent work, his kiln was flourishing while his brother almost brought to ruin the better kiln. Stirred up by his wife, the younger brother went to his elder brother's kiln at midnight, trying to destroy it out of jealousy. He sneaked into his elder brother's workshop and dumped loess, bricks and other miscellaneous things into the glaze vat and stirred them up hard for giving vent to his depressed and discontented feelings. Unexpectedly, the elder brother produced a kiln of ceramics with beautiful multicolored glaze without knowing the cause and had no idea how to repeat the unexpected success. Afterwards, the younger brother was repentant of his fault and started to study hard the technique of multicolored glaze. After numerous failures, he finally succeeded and burned the brilliant multicolored glaze that looked like floating clouds and flowing water, resplendent with variegated coloration.

# Origin of Bowl Bottom

In the past, an emperor took a fancy to the celadon bowl produced in the Cizhouyao Kiln very much but he hated the bowl bottom that burned his hand when holding it so he ordered pottery artisans to improve porcelain bowls not burning hand in ten days. A pottery artisan named Wan'er took the task on his own initiative. When ears were added, the bowl became a jar; and when a handle was added, it became a pot. Neither way helped to solve the problem. One night when he was so sleepy that he fell asleep, the candle burned the collar of his ragged cotton-padded coat. His mother came over trying to stamp out the fire but the more she stamped, the higher the flame went. When waking up with a start, Wan'er found his mother standing on his burning coat with her soles smoking. In a grasp, he carried his mother to the edge of the *kang* (bed) and took off her shoes. To his great surprise, he found that neither her feet nor her shoes were burned because of the wooden soles studded at the bottom of the shoes. Inspired by the wood-bottomed shoes, Wan'er succeeded in working out a bowl with a pad that very night so that when one held the bowl the hand would not be burned. Afterwards, other pottery artisans thought the solid bowl bottom was too heavy and not good-looking either so they used a ring-shaped bottom instead to achieve a better effect of thermal isolation.

The legend has another version in the locality. In the Ming Dynasty, when passing by Pengcheng, the king of the Yan State took a liking to the glittering flowered bowl but his hand was burned by its bottom when holding it. Thus he issued an order to have a bowl made within five days that would not burn the hand. Nie Wansan, a superb handicraftsman in the town, accepted the task. At night, on seeing the crescent against a faint cloud, oblate in shape, he got an inspiration. The idea struck him was that if two crescent-shaped clay strips were stuck to the bottom of the bowl, they would help to isolate the heat to a certain extent and the hand holding it would not be burned. Henceforth, the bowl of Pengcheng had a bottom. Later, other pottery artisans changed the two separated clay strips into a ring so that the effect of thermal isolation was much improved.

## Origin of Wax Printing

The people living in many Miao nationality areas in China are still singing an ancient song "The Song of Wax Printing" about the origin of wax printing. Long long ago, according to a legend, a clever and beautiful Miao nationality girl was discontented with single-colored clothes and hoped to print various beautiful flower-and-plant patterns on her skirt. However, the craft of that time could only paint patterns by hand on skirts one by one. She was at a loss what to do and felt depressed. One day, on gazing at the hills full of fresh flowers, the girl was absorbed in meditation and fell into a trance, sinking into a deep sleep. In obscurity, a flower fairy, beautifully-dressed, took her to a garden with singing birds and fragrant flowers, dancing butterflies and busy-working bees. The girl was so fascinated by the beautiful scene that she had no idea at all about those bees crawling on her dress. When coming to her senses, she saw those spots and stains of honey and wax left on her clothes. Putting her coat and skirt into a bucket for dyeing indigo, she tried to dye them once again so as to cover the wax stains. After dyeing, the girl put her dress into boiling water to rinse out the floating color. When she took out the clothes, a miracle occurred before her eyes. Beautiful white flowers appeared on the dark blue coat and skirt where they had been stained with wax! A bright idea occurred to her. At once, she took some wax and melted it by heating first and then drew some flower patterns on a piece of white cloth with a twig. After that it was dyed in indigo liquid and finally when the wax was melted away by boiling water, white flower patterns appeared on the cloth. The girl was so happy that she sang a folk song. On hearing the resounding song, the countrymen, far and near, all came to see the skirt with flower patterns she had dyed and learned from her the skill of how to draw flowers and patterns on cloth. With this skill they dyed a great variety of cloth. From this time on, the technique of wax printing has been spread and handed down in the Miao nationality and the other fraternal national minorities living together with them such as the Bouyi nationality, the Yao nationality, etc.

# Bodiless Lacquer Ware Created by Shen Shaoan

During the Qianlong regime in the Qing Dynasty, there was an ordinary lacquerer named Shen Shaoan running a shop by the Shuangpao Bridge. He was engaged mainly in lacquer painting but also in making small commodities like lacquer ware, lacquer bowl, memorial wood tablet, etc. As his business was slack, Shen Shaoan often went to those imposing dwellings and spacious courtyards of officials and officers or Taoist temples and Buddhist temples to do lacquer painting work. Once when he was working in an ancient temple, he found the wood of the horizontal inscribed board of the temple at the entrance had already rotten but the body inside mounted with lacquered linen was still intact. Shen Shaoan was a man careful enough to get some inspiration from it. He first molded figurines, flowers, birds or utensils with clay and then coated them with lacquered linen or silk fabric layer by layer. When the fabrics coated with lacquer on the mold were parched, he drilled a hole at the bottom of the mold and then immersed it into water to dissolve the clay body. The last step of this workmanship was to polish the hardened fabric shell and to coat it with different colors of lacquer. Thus the bodiless lacquer ware was made. Shen Shaoan became the earliest artisan to make bodiless lacquer ware in Fuzhou. It has found favor in everybody's eyes for its advantages, hollow in body, light in weight, artistic in looking and durable in use. From then on, the bodiless lacqureware of Fuzhou, together with the cloisonné enamel of Beijing and the ceramics of Jingdezhen, Jiangxi, are called "the three treasured objects of the traditional arts and crafts of China."

*The Book of Changes* completed in the Zhou Dynasty already raised a statement to the effect that a large number of articles beneficial to national welfare and the people's livelihood were created by sages, expressing the viewpoint that all articles were created by sages and all workmanships were for the purpose of use. The *You Xue Qiong Lin* (an enlightened reading material widely circulating among the people at the turn of the Ming Dynasty and the Qing Dynasty) explained the beauty of utensils, skills and arts and crafts like this, "It seems that unusual skills are unbeneficial to people while handicrafts are helpful to practical purposes." The idea at its core is also to lay emphasis on practical purposes and uses.

The legends about folk arts and crafts are also obviously affected by the idea that the perfection of utensils is not the ultimate end and that only when a utensil serves the purpose of use can it be said to have attained the realm of a lofty state. Of course, it is also related to the form of passing on and carrying on the ancient arts and crafts of China. The traditional way of passing on skills in China was basically the form of training an apprentice by his master. However, due to the conservative ideas of handicraft trade, masters would often hold back some crafts with higher technique so as to ensure the continuance of their own means of livelihood. Therefore, the legends about crafts and arts were always lifted up to the height of trade worship. So far as learners concerned, their psychology was not only learning from their masters and believing what their master taught them. They also had a prostrating psychology of begging for skills, supplicating for patronage and praying for good luck. Those heroes or heroines in the legend making creation or improvement in some workmanship were often adored as the founder of the trade.

The ideas of practical use and technology for all handicrafts can be said as two wings full of tensile force and the essence of the traditional culture of China as well. The handicraft culture in the legends, as an important component part of the traditional culture of China, embodies lively the ideas of practical use for all handicrafts and skills. In the vast world of the utensils for people's everyday use, these ideas have produced a wide and far-reaching effect on the traditional viewpoint of the Chinese people.

# Appendix: A Brief Chronology of China

| | |
|---|---|
| Paleolithic Period | c. 1.7 million-10,000 years ago |
| Neolithic Age | c. 10,000-4,000 years ago |
| Xia Dynasty | 2070-1600 B.C. |
| Shang Dynasty | 1600-1046 B.C. |
| Western Zhou Dynasty | 1046-771 B.C. |
| Spring and Autumn Period | 770-476 B.C. |
| Warring States Period | 475-221 B.C. |
| Qin Dynasty | 221-206 B.C. |
| Western Han Dynasty | 206 B.C.-A.D. 25 |
| Eastern Han Dynasty | 25-220 |
| Three Kingdoms | 220-280 |
| Western Jin Dynasty | 265-317 |
| Eastern Jin Dynasty | 317-420 |
| Northern and Southern Dynasty | 420-589 |
| Sui Dynasty | 581-618 |
| Tang Dynasty | 618-907 |
| Five Dynasties | 907-960 |
| Northern Song Dynasty | 960-1127 |
| Southern Song Dynasty | 1127-1279 |
| Liao Dynasty | 907-1125 |
| Jin Dynasty | 1115-1234 |
| Yuan Dynasty | 1206-1368 |
| Ming Dynasty | 1368-1644 |
| Qing Dynasty | 1616-1911 |